A TEST OF CRICKET

KNOW THE GAME

A TEST OF CRICKET
KNOW THE GAME

Mike Atherton

WITH PAT GIBSON

Hodder & Stoughton

ACKNOWLEDGMENTS

I would like to express my sincere thanks to Pat Gibson for tirelessly helping me to produce this book. He even flew to Australia in order to keep me to the schedule. I would also like to thank Patrick Eagar and Graham Morris for the excellent photographs. Finally, I would like to thank my publisher Roddy Bloomfield for his advice and encouragement at all times.

First published in Great Britain in 1995 by
Hodder and Stoughton
A division of Hodder Headline Plc

British Library Cataloguing in Publication Data

Atherton, Mike
  Test of Cricket: Know the Game
  I. Title
  796.358

ISBN 0-340-63775-7

Printed and bound in Great Britain by
Scotprint Ltd., Musselburgh

Hodder and Stoughton
A division of Hodder Headline Plc
338 Euston Road
London NW1 3BH

CONTENTS

1 WHAT IS CRICKET?

When someone asked the great Louis Armstrong to define jazz, he replied: 'Man, if you've gotta ask, you'll never know.' You could say the same about cricket but here goes...

There are actually two definitions of 'cricket' in *Chambers English Dictionary*. One is 'a saltatory, orthopterous insect, allied to grasshoppers and locusts'. The other is 'an outdoor game played with bats, a ball, and wickets, between two sides of eleven each'. I will concentrate on the more complicated of the two.

As Andrew Lang, a Scotsman who ought to have been a cricket writer since he wrote about almost everything from history to fairy tales, once observed: 'No one invented cricket. Like almost everything else, cricket was evolved.' But the historians tell us that it began as early as the seventh or eighth century in the fields of southern England where shepherds would pass the time by playing a kind of bat-and-ball game.

Apparently the name of the game comes from the Anglo-Saxon word *cricce* which was a curved wooden staff. The shepherds would use their staffs to defend their 'wicket' gates topped by a crossbar or 'bail' against a stone or some such object thrown towards them.

From those humble beginnings has grown a game of skill and tactics which has developed from a simple pastime into an international sport generating millions of pounds. The best players represent their countries in five-day 'Test' matches – so-called because they are the ultimate *test* of cricket ability – and in a one-day tournament for the World Cup, which is staged every four years.

It is at times like these that everyone becomes an expert – apart from the England captain who is held in as high esteem as a failed football manager or a chairman of a privatised public utility when things are going wrong, which has been depressingly often in recent years.

In such circumstances, this may seem a bit rich coming from me but I wonder how much these 'experts' know, how much they understand, in the immortal words of Fred Trueman, 'just what is going off out there.'

THE BASICS

The basics are simple enough. It is 'an outdoor game played with bats, a ball, and wickets, between two sides of eleven each'. They take it in turns to bat and bowl on a PITCH twenty-two yards long set in the middle of a field with a boundary marked by a white line or a rope seventy-five yards away. At either end of the pitch stands a WICKET – three vertical stumps connected at the top by two horizontal pieces called bails. Three CREASES are also marked – the *bowling* crease in line with the stumps, the *popping* crease four feet in front of it, and the *return* crease at each end of the bowling crease and at right angles to it. The bowler must bowl the ball from between the return crease and the wicket with some part of his front foot behind the popping crease. Six deliveries from one end to the other constitute an OVER at the end of which a different bowler delivers another over from the other end.

A batsman scores RUNS by hitting the ball into the field and crossing from one end to the other before any member of the fielding side can throw it back and dislodge the wicket. If the ball reaches the boundary, the batsman automatically scores four runs. If it crosses the boundary without touching the ground, he scores six runs.

A batsman can be OUT in many different ways: BOWLED if he misses the ball and it strikes the wicket; CAUGHT if he hits the ball in the air and a fielder catches it; STUMPED or RUN OUT if he does not have his foot or bat grounded inside the popping crease when a wicketkeeper or fielder breaks the wicket with the ball; LEG BEFORE WICKET if part of his body stops a delivery from hitting the stumps; HIT WICKET if he dislodges the stumps himself. He can also be out for HITTING THE BALL TWICE, for HANDLING THE BALL or for OBSTRUCTING THE FIELD, which are fairly self-explanatory. And he can be TIMED OUT if he does not step on to the field of play within two minutes of the previous batsman being dismissed.

When ten of the eleven batsmen are out, the INNINGS is completed and the other team takes its turn to bat. Matches can consist of one or two innings per side with the team scoring most runs winning the game. If the scores are level on completion of the innings, the result is called a TIE. If the match is not completed because of the weather, which happens quite often in Manchester, or because the teams have run out of time, the result is a DRAW.

Simple, isn't it? Only there is a lot more to it than that. Let me try to explain who does what, why they do it – and how, in some cases, I think they could do it better.

**❝ A Bat, a Ball, two Wickets and a Field –
What words are these that can such magic yield!❞**

GEORGE FRANCIS WILSON, poet

CAPTAINCY

2 PICKING A TEAM

The first task facing a captain is to pick the team which, unless you are an autocrat like W. G. Grace or just happen to own the club, the ground and the bats and balls as well, means reaching a consensus with the committee responsible for the selection process.

There have been times in the past when it has been a relatively straightforward matter. Fixtures like Smokers v. Non-smokers, Married v. Single, One Arm v. One Leg and Ugly Men v. Handsome Men, which are just some of the strange matches which can be found in the cricket records, did narrow down the choice a little.

Normally, however, it is more complicated than that – and especially when it comes to picking a Test side. Sir Donald Bradman, who knew all about it as both captain and chairman of selectors, once wrote: 'A selector's job is interesting, sometimes exasperating, occasionally heartbreaking.' I know what he meant although I hope that the present English system will keep the exasperation and the heartbreak to a minimum – and not just among the selectors.

THE ENGLISH WAY

We now have a four-man committee which in 1995 comprised the chairman, Ray Illingworth, two more elected selectors, David Graveney and Fred Titmus, and myself. I think our meetings were good value. They were open, honest and forthright. As captain, I had a say and though it was less of a say than some previous captains had, I was happy with it.

ADVANTAGE

As a twenty-six-year-old captain without that much Test match experience, I could look to older heads to pass on their knowledge and act as a counterbalance to what you could call my youthful naïveté. The selectors also saw more county cricket than I did and

The England selectors in 1994 – Fred Titmus, Brian Bolus and chairman Ray Illingworth. With them are Alan Smith, chief executive of the Test and County Cricket Board, left, and former England off-spinner John Emburey, right.

were therefore in a better position to make cricketing judgments. What generally happened was that we would pick twelve or thirteen players to report for the Test match and then the choice of the final eleven would be left to my preference, my gut feeling on the matter, if you like.

DISADVANTAGE

The captain may not always be happy with the final eleven he is given but, on balance, I think our system is the best one. It is certainly preferable to a captain having an all-pervasive influence and most certainly preferable to a captain having no say at all.

THE AUSTRALIAN WAY

The Australians prefer a system which is the complete opposite of ours in that their Test teams and touring parties are selected by a committee which does not include either the captain or the coach, who fulfils much the same role as our manager. I think the captain must have the ear of the chairman of selectors because I cannot believe that his views are totally ignored, but he does not have a vote.

ADVANTAGE

The Australians are convinced that this helps the captain to work better with his players, both on the pitch and in the dressing room. It certainly helped Allan Border through some tough times when they were losing regularly in the early stages of his captaincy in the eighties. He always had the ultimate fallback position of saying that

The rest of the 1994 selection committee – captain and team manager, Keith Fletcher.

he did not pick the team but just captained the players the selectors gave him. I am sure that when a side is having a rough time, the fact that the buck does not stop with the captain eases the pressure on him and makes for more continuity.

DISADVANTAGE

Problems arise when the captain is totally against the selectors' decision – as Border was when they left out Geoff Marsh, his vice-captain, friend and confidant.

COUNTY CRICKET

Different counties have different ways of doing things, with much depending on the roles of the captain and manager or coach. In recent times, my own club, Lancashire, has provided a perfect example of the two extremes. For the two years that Neil Fairbrother was captain, he was solely responsible for picking the team. Certain people like David Hughes, the manager, myself as vice-captain, and some of the senior players had his ear and he would seek and take advice from us. But there was no selection committee as such and he had the final say. When Michael Watkinson took over the captaincy, Lancashire adopted a completely different system. Now, there is a selection committee, consisting of the captain himself, the vice-captain, the coach, David Lloyd, and two vastly experienced members of the cricket committee, Clive Lloyd and Jack Simmons, and we all have a say.

The wheel had gone full circle and it highlighted the dilemma over the manager's position in English cricket. In football, it is patently obvious where the buck stops. The manager is responsible for the team's performance, he takes the flak if things go wrong and he is ultimately judged on the success or failure of his side. In cricket, the situation is nothing like as clear. The majority of the decisions that matter are taken on the field and there it is the captain, not the manager, who is in charge.

Lancashire's experience exposed one of the major problems. David Hughes had been a very successful captain, a strong leader who controlled the dressing room and disliked interference from outside. When he became manager, he was caught between two stools. He had little say in team selection and little influence on the captain, largely, I am sure, of his own volition. Yet he was ultimately held responsible for the side's lack of success and decided to leave the club.

Under the new system, that responsibility now rests with the captain. The coach is there to help in any way he can but his responsibilities are solely in a coaching, advisory and selectorial capacity. Lancashire believe that this is the best way to bring success to the club but elsewhere in English cricket the debate goes on. Some counties like Durham, Northamptonshire and Surrey have directors of cricket in Geoff Cook, Phil Neale and Mike Edwards; others such as Essex, Hampshire and Middlesex have had hugely influential captains in Graham Gooch, Mark Nicholas and Mike Gatting who worked closely with their coaches and committees but more or less ran things their way.

My view is that if you have a captain who is worth his salt, controls the dressing room and knows what he is doing on the field, all he needs is a well-respected former player in a coaching and advisory role. The captain should have as much help as possible but his is the ultimate responsibility.

" My God, look what they've given me this time. "

Lancashire's ARCHIE MACLAREN, who succeeded W. G. Grace as England captain and never won a series in ten years

---

If you think that the England selectors have a difficult job in picking from eighteen counties, consider the problems of their counterparts in the West Indies. Cricket is the only thing that unites the countries of the Caribbean yet the fierce inter-island rivalry can make selection very political. When the West Indies played South Africa in one of the most historic Tests of all time in Barbados, only a handful of spectators turned up because, it was supposed, Anderson Cummins, the Bajan fast bowler, had not been picked.

Then, when we played in the Caribbean in 1994, there were strong feelings around the islands that politics had influenced the selection of the young Guyanese left-hander Shivnarine Chanderpaul for the second Test in Georgetown. Guyana has a large Indian population and it was felt that 'Chandra' had been picked in preference to Trinidad's Phil Simmons to placate the locals and encourage their attendance.

3 THE BALANCED SIDE

Whoever is responsible for picking the team, the ideal is to come up with a balanced side, always assuming that the pitch you are going to play on will provide a fair contest between bat and ball. My idea of the perfect balance would comprise five good batsmen, an all-rounder good enough to bat at number six *and* be one of the front-line seamers, a wicketkeeper-batsman, two spinners – one an off-spinner, the other either a leg-spinner or a slow left armer – a swing bowler and an out-and-out fast bowler. Unfortunately such a side is easier to produce on paper than it is to take on to the field.

I know it is what Ray Illingworth had in mind when he took over

(OPPOSITE, TOP)*Alan Knott, an all-rounder in his own right.*

Four great all-rounders (BELOW, LEFT TO RIGHT) *Ian Botham, Sir Richard Hadlee, Imran Khan, Kapil Dev.*

as chairman of the England selectors. He wanted a side like the ones he used to lead in the early seventies, a side which would provide runs all the way down the batting order and still offer plenty of variety of bowling. The key was that England had a number of outstanding all-rounders – Basil d'Oliveira, Tony Greig, Ray himself – plus a wicketkeeper in Alan Knott who was such an effective batsman that he could also be considered an all-rounder in his own right.

We are not so well off these days. You cannot pursue the idea of a balanced side if you haven't got the resources available. And England have had to face the fact that since Ian Botham left the international scene they have not had an all-rounder who could score Test match centuries and take five wickets in an innings – though, hopefully, the emergence of Dominic Cork in 1995 will hugely strengthen us in this department.

Not that we are alone in this respect. Cricket and cricket-lovers around the world were spoiled in the seventies and eighties when there was a flush of great all-rounders. Apart from Botham, there were Imran Khan, Kapil Dev and Sir Richard Hadlee, all absolutely

superb cricketers who were able to turn a game with either bat or ball. But they have all gone now. That era is over and sides are having to make the best of what they have got. They are looking at other ways to balance the side – to wicketkeepers who can bat, like Australia's Ian Healy and England's Jack Russell; to batsmen who can bowl, like Australia's Steve and Mark Waugh, England's Graeme Hick and the West Indies' Carl Hooper; and to bowlers who can make a few runs, like England's Dominic Cork, Phillip DeFreitas and Darren Gough.

In the absence of the great all-rounders, the modern approach to Test match cricket is to play six batsmen and four bowlers, providing that one or two of the batsmen can bowl a little and come on and do a 'bits and pieces' job throughout the course of a match. With this kind of selection, a team will try to get a big score – 400, 500, even 600 – on the board and then play the pressure game, grinding the opposition into the ground with tight bowling and fielding and hoping they will crack. Most current Test sides adopt this approach and Australia have been particularly successful with it. They have had the advantage of having the Waugh twins, Mark and Steve, who are both useful bowlers as well as being high-class batsmen, and a wicketkeeper like Healy who has scored a lot of invaluable runs.

They have also had Shane Warne and all his variations to help them offset the downside of this policy, which is that the bowling can sometimes lack variety and leave the captain without too many options. To win Test matches, you have to bowl the other side out twice, you have to take twenty wickets, and the more options the captain has the better.

For our part, England have had to accept that Ian Botham was not replaceable by any one player. They tried over the years with people like Derek Pringle, David Capel and Chris Lewis but none of them could really fill Ian's boots and now we have accepted the reality of the situation. In the mid 'nineties, the only all-rounder in English cricket whose batting was of Test class was Craig White, the only all-rounders whose bowling was up to Test standard was Dominic Cork and, at his best, Chris Lewis. So we had to look for other ways to replace Ian and one of Ray Illingworth's major requirements was bowlers who can also score runs.

This meant that when we picked the side to go to Australia in 1994–5, it was considered that we had a strong batting line-up, a powerful battery of seam bowlers and at least one experienced spinner. We also had an excellent wicketkeeper-batsman in Steve Rhodes, who had performed so admirably since getting into the Test

Jack Russell, who returned in 1995 to take a pivotal role in the England side.

team the previous summer that his poor showing in Australia was a major blow. Fortunately for us, Jack Russell was playing better than he had ever done and after returning to the side against the West Indies in 1995 he had an outstanding tour of South Africa. His was the pivotal role, batting at number seven and giving the side plenty of buzz in the field.

On top of that we were looking for the bowlers to score runs. DeFreitas and Gough always fancy themselves with the bat anyway and their batting has certainly been influential in some of our better

THE GREAT ALL-ROUNDERS

	Tests	Runs	Wickets
Kapil Dev	131	5,284 (31·05)	434 (29·62)
Ian Botham	102	5,200 (33·54)	383 (28·40)
Imran Khan	88	3,807 (37·69)	362 (22·81)
Sir Richard Hadlee	86	3,124 (27·16)	431 (22·29)

performances in recent times. Between them, they transformed the Oval Test against South Africa in 1994; the tail, marshalled by Darren, saw us past 300 and on to a psychological high at Sydney in 1995; and Daffy's 88 was crucial to our subsequent victory at Adelaide. The days are gone when tail-enders can get away with being absolute 'rabbits' and to this end we always make sure that all our bowlers undergo some serious batting practice in the nets in the two days before a Test match. I don't make too many hard and fast rules when it comes to practice because it is better to allow people to prepare in the way which suits them best. But one thing I do insist on is compulsory nets for all the bowlers.

Batsmen who can bowl and bowlers who can bat are just as important, if not more so, in limited-overs cricket. All the good one-day sides I have known have had a lot of all-rounders. Lancashire again provide a good example with people like Wasim Akram, Phillip DeFreitas, Mike Watkinson and Ian Austin in the side which won the Sunday League in 1989 and completed the Benson and Hedges Cup–NatWest double a year later. And it is because of the all-round ability of players like DeFreitas, Lewis, Cork, Gough, Rhodes and Hick that over the years England have had one of the best one-day sides.

Not that this should be a consideration when it comes to picking touring sides. There is more scope for variety because you are usually taking at least sixteen players but I believe they should always be selected with the Test matches in mind. The best Test players are invariably good enough to adapt to one-day cricket but the reverse is not necessarily true. Indeed there have been a number of cases of players who have been successful in one-day cricket but have struggled to make the grade in Test cricket.

Finally, having stressed the desirability of picking a balanced side, I should point out that it is not always practicable. If you look at

66 My attitude to cricket is that when I'm bowling there's no one in the world good enough to bat against me and when I'm batting there's no one good enough to bowl at me. 99

IAN BOTHAM

Phillip DeFreitas, a
bowler who can bat.

India's success against England in 1992–3, it was based on a policy
of playing two seamers and three spinners, thereby utilising an
'unbalanced' attack to take advantage of their proven strength on
their own pitches. The West Indies, on the other hand, dominated
Test cricket for more than a decade by playing four fast bowlers – a
policy which England used with success when we beat South Africa
at the Oval in 1994.

ON BALANCE

Alec Bedser, England's longest-serving chairman of selectors, maintains that Sir Donald Bradman's 1948 Australians was the best-balanced side he ever saw. 'They had everything really,' he says. 'A lot of very good batsmen, all-rounders, pace bowlers, off-spin, leg-spin, a high-class wicketkeeper and outstanding fielders.' At full strength, it read:

Sid Barnes	Sam Loxton
Arthur Morris	Ray Lindwall
Don Bradman	Don Tallon
Lindsay Hassett	Bill Johnston
Neil Harvey	Ian Johnson or Doug Ring
Keith Miller	

Personally, I believe Mark Taylor's 1994–5 Australians took a lot of beating when it came to balance. Take this side:

Mark Taylor	Ian Healy
Michael Slater	Shane Warne
David Boon	Tim May
Mark Waugh	Craig McDermott
Michael Bevan	Damien Fleming
Steve Waugh	

The batting provided a nice mix of aggression and patience with a left-hand/right-hand opening combination, a left-hander (Bevan) in the middle-order and a wicketkeeper who can bat. The attack consisted of a fast bowler, a swing bowler, a leg-spinner and an off-spinner plus the Waugh twins to fill in with seamers.

4 CHARACTERS AND LIFESTYLES

Cricket is a team game played by eleven individuals. The team ethic is vitally important but a captain must also recognise and try to accommodate the different characters, the different tastes and the different kinds of lifestyles within his team. The best teams are those in which the whole adds up to more than the eleven constituent parts.

Graham Gooch, my predecessor as England captain, was often criticised by the media for throwing a kind of blanket over the eleven individuals in his team or the sixteen in a tour party, expecting them all to do the same kind of training, to adopt the same practice methods and to accept the same sort of discipline as he did. While this was very much an over-simplification, it was regarded as such because Graham wanted to bring a greater degree of professionalism to the England side and to that end flair and individuality sometimes had to be bypassed.

I was interested to read the thoughts of Bobby Simpson, the Australian coach, on the subject soon after we had picked the side to go to Australia in 1994–5. In a column in the *Daily Express*, he said that the Australians always preferred to play against an England team including people like Ian Botham, Allan Lamb and David Gower because they reckoned that they were a disparate force within that team. He felt that, because of their presence, the England team was never as united, as together, as his own touring side.

My own views on this are a) that it is obviously much easier to be together when you are part of a touring team and b) that all players are different and it is wrong to expect them to train and practise the same way.

Look at Phil Tufnell and Devon Malcolm, for example. They have completely different bodies for a start, one spindly with very little muscle, the other powerful and very heavily built. They also do completely different jobs. Devon may have to charge up to the wicket in short, explosive bursts for twenty overs in a day while Tuffers may be asked to bowl thirty beguiling overs in one or two spells.

As far as I am concerned, a strong team ethic is crucial to the success of the side. We want superstars, of course we do, but not at the expense of the team framework and ethos. We want everybody to muck in and do the right thing. But, equally, you have to accept people for who they are and what they are and, when the time is right, let them go off and do their own things.

An example of this was the way I attempted to treat Phil Tufnell in the West Indies in 1994 when I tried to give him as much leeway, as much rope, as he could reasonably expect. I felt that what was of paramount importance, and in the best interests of the side, was to get Phil to bowl to the best of his ability when it counted, i.e. on the match days. My view was that we would best get that by giving him as much freedom off the field as possible and not 'mothering' him so much in practice.

In India the previous winter, he performed poorly for his country. This may or may not have had something to do with the approach of the management on that tour. Some of his behaviour, particularly at Vishakhapatnam, was poor but at the same time the reaction was, I felt, somewhat heavy-handed.

As things turned out, he bowled well in the West Indies. He only played in a couple of Tests but when he did play he bowled well. I think there may have been occasions when I gave him too much leeway, to the detriment of one or two other members of the side who felt he was being afforded special treatment. But the intention, as ever, was with the best interests of the side at heart. Whether it worked or not is for other people to judge.

LIFESTYLES

Before anyone runs away with the idea that Phil Tufnell is the only England cricketer with his own way of doing things, I should tell you about a few more with their own individual characteristics and lifestyles which the captain has to take into account.

Like Tuffers, Robin Smith is an active socialite. They are both very gregarious and dislike being cooped up in their hotel rooms. They like to be out and about, having a drink, having a laugh, and in many ways their sociability can be good for the atmosphere in the dressing room.

At the other extreme, we have Jack Russell, who is very intense about his cricket. He is almost a recluse on tour, holing himself up in his room or going out painting and only putting in an appearance at the training ground or when he is actually playing. He is an avid practiser and a deep thinker about the game who is very analytical and self-critical. There is nothing wrong with that kind of attitude in the dressing room, either.

Then we have someone like Darren Gough who is very upbeat and positive, believing that he is capable of doing anything. That is a

Phillip Tufnell – a case for special treatment.

very healthy outlook which you would never want to take away from his cricket. His youthful exuberance is totally beneficial to the side but sometimes you have to temper it slightly.

At this early stage of his career, Darren is receptive to advice, but

Darren Gough –
youthful exuberance.

other, more senior bowlers can be more temperamental. Phillip DeFreitas, for example, is a new-ball bowler and proud of it. And he is a much better bowler when the captain gives him the end he wants, lets him have the advantage of the wind and makes him feel that he is the No. 1 bowler in the side. In the interests of the side you are better off giving him what he wants even if it amounts to pampering him a little. As for Angus Fraser, you always know when he is bowling that he will never want to come off, so it is pointless asking him if he wants one more over or two. He just wants to bowl.

All a captain can do is take all these things into consideration and try to get the best out of everybody. Sometimes it works; sometimes it doesn't. On the last West Indian tour, we had two batsmen, Mark Ramprakash and Nasser Hussain, who are very intense and very uptight about their cricket precisely because they are so desperate to do well. I tried to get them to relax and play their natural games when they were playing for England. Nasser, to be fair to him, did not have too many opportunities but 'Ramps' did. In fact he played very well in the island games but he did not do particularly well in the Test matches so I cannot say that I had any great success in that endeavour.

ONE OF THE BOYS?

A question that is often asked is: can a captain be one of the boys? My answer is that I think he can – to a degree.

When Graham Gooch was captain, I think the England players were somewhat in awe of him at times, partly because of the age difference between him and the rest of the side and partly because he was still far and away the outstanding player in the team.

When I became captain I was only twenty-five and therefore younger than many of the other players, and I was by no means the best player in the team. With this in mind, I hoped that the rest of the guys might find it easier to relate to me and easier to communicate with me. Again, it is not for me to say whether or not this has happened.

There are times when a captain has to distance himself from the other players whether he likes it or not. While you may feel like one of the boys, having a drink with them and sharing their interests, you still have to be prepared to hand out the rollickings when they are necessary. I don't like doing it and I have only had to do it on a couple of occasions but you have to be seen to be strong enough to take what is very much a captain's responsibility.

Just how far a captain should distance himself from the rest of the team is entirely up to him. At Old Trafford, where Lancashire still operate under a very hierarchical system, there is a capped players' dressing room, an uncapped players' dressing room – and a captain's room. And it was interesting that when David Hughes became captain, he took the captain's room. He wanted that distance between himself and the players, that aloofness if you like, because he felt that the club had been in a poor state and needed some discipline imposed on it. To do this, he was prepared to make himself unpopular by moving away from the rest of the lads. When he was succeeded first by Neil Fairbrother and then by Mike Watkinson, both of them stayed in the main dressing room. As with so many things in cricket, different people have different ways of doing things.

GETTING IT TOGETHER

The more I am involved in team selection, the more I take account of the character of the players under consideration. Whether we are picking a team for a home Test or a party for a tour, I want people who dearly want to play – and win – for England, people who are not going to give up in adversity.

More and more, the selectors need to look past the obvious. There is a need to look beyond mere batting and bowling statistics to the kind of temperament a player has and, in effect, how much 'bottle' he has. Allan Border and the Australian selectors took this attitude during the mid 1980s when Australia were in the doldrums. After some failures in the early part of his captaincy, Border came to the conclusion that they could sacrifice some extra skill for commitment, desire and a love of playing for your country.

I also want people – and this applies especially on tour – who are not going to be a disruptive influence, people who are not going to sulk and whine when they are not actually playing but give a hundred per cent support to the players who are.

Fortunately there are not too many disruptive influences about because most cricketers are pretty genial, fairly philosophical blokes. But, as a captain, the only time I would consider a player who might cause a bit of trouble and unsettle the side is if it was felt that he was going to be a match-winner. If they are not going to win matches for you, players like that are not worth having around.

5 UNDERSTANDING PITCHES

Cricket is more dependent on the playing surface than any other sport. It dictates team selection, the balance of the side, whether you want to bat or bowl first, even the kind of cricket that is going to be played.

That is why the pitch is the subject of so much attention before, during and after a match. You will see players and officials prodding and poking it, journalists making prognostications about it and spectators gazing at it in awe as though it is one of the wonders of the universe. But what are they looking for?

First, it is important to understand the effect of different pitches on the behaviour of the ball.

Conditions for seam

For the ball to 'seam', that is for it to deviate one way or the other when the vertical seam or stitching around the ball lands on the pitch, there has to be plenty of grass, preferably 'live' grass, which, when you rub it with your thumb or scuff it with your bat, will leave a greenish mark. If the grass is dead, the ball might not seam at all – as Mike Gatting found to his cost when Lancashire played Middlesex at Old Trafford in 1992. The pitch was covered in about two inches of grass and Mike put us in but we made 456 for 3 declared. The grass which had tempted him turned out to be dead grass which meant that the wicket was fast and true and the ball went straight through.

I erred the other way when I won the toss and batted first against Western Australia at Perth in 1994. There wasn't that much grass but the grass which was there was juicy and 'live' and conditions were extremely favourable to seam and swing bowling in the first session.

Pitches will also seam if there are cracks which are sometimes so extensive and pronounced that the surface takes the form of a mosaic. When the edges of the cracks are unstable and move about when you touch them, or when they show signs of crumbling, there is a good chance that the ball will seam off those edges. It will also bounce at varying heights and become 'up and down', as we call it. But, again, first impressions can be misleading. Sometimes you come across pitches which are really cracked but, because the edges remain firm, offer very little help to the seam. I have known pitches at Melbourne and Sabina Park, Jamaica, where the surface looked awful but because the cracks held firm there was very little movement at all.

Conditions for swing

Despite years of scientific study, in the field, in wind tunnels and pressure chambers, there are still no hard and fast rules for deciding when the ball is going to swing or swerve in the air. The conventional wisdom is that atmospheric forces cause the ball to move laterally, with a heavy atmosphere acting on a ball which is shiny on one side and rough on the other having the greatest effect. In theory, you need warmish weather, plenty of moisture in the air and a bit of dampness in the pitch. A nice cross-breeze is also beneficial. The ball is not expected to swing if there is bright sunshine and not a cloud in the sky or on a fresh windy day with little humidity in the air. But you can never be sure. Sometimes you think the ball is going to swing and it doesn't; sometimes you think it won't swing and it does. Headingley fooled us all when England played South Africa in 1994. The pitch seemed a bit damp, the atmosphere was humid and everyone thought that the ball was bound to swing, especially for a bowler like Fanie de Villiers, but it hardly moved off the straight all day.

A relatively new phenomenon is what is known as 'reverse-swing' which, as the name implies, is the exact opposite of the accepted practice. For this, you also need conditions which are in complete contrast to what you require for normal swing bowling. The pitch needs to be hard and grassless and the outfield dry and dusty so that the ball will become scuffed. By keeping one side shiny and the other rough, the ball will swing in reverse to its usual direction.

Conditions for spin

For the ball to turn one way or the other, you need a surface on which it is going to grip. Traditionally, this will be a soil pitch which will become looser the longer the game goes on, or, in hot countries like India and Pakistan, become so baked and crusty that cracks and holes will appear in it. The spinner wants a pitch that is going to break up, either on the main part of the wicket through general wear and tear, or in the rough caused by the bowlers following through on or just outside the line of the stumps.

READING THE SIGNS

It is a fact of cricket life that conditions vary from ground to ground and country to country so it is a great help if you have been there before or you can discuss the pitch's characteristics with someone who has. But there are still a number of things you want to find out for yourself and certain points which you tick off on a kind of check list in assessing what you are going to do if you win the toss.

First you want to know whether there is grass on the pitch and whether it is 'live' or 'dead' because that should determine whether the ball is going to seam. Then you want to find out whether the pitch is hard, which you can do either by standing on it with your studs or pressing a key into the ground near the pitch, as Tony Greig and Geoff Boycott do in their television pitch reports before a Test match. If the key does not go in, it indicates that the pitch is firm and quick; if the key does go in, it suggests that the pitch is slow or, perhaps, that it is damp underneath. In which case the ball may grip and seam.

You want to know how much the pitch is going to wear so you look to see if there are any cracks in it. If they move when you touch them, it is likely that they will crumble at the edges, leading to unevenness in bounce and, perhaps, turn later on. If there are no cracks, or if the ones there feel firm and solid, the chances are that the bounce will remain true.

You will talk to the groundsman (or the curator, as they call him in Australia) because he has probably worked on the pitch for years and knows its idiosyncrasies better than anybody – although you must also remember that he does not always get it right himself.

Before a particular one-day international, I asked the groundsman what the pitch would be like and he said it would be hard, fast and true, staying like that throughout the game and producing plenty of runs. In actual fact, it turned out to be exactly the opposite – a low, slow turner which got worse as the game wore on.

Finally you look at the conditions overhead. At a ground like Headingley, the weather can be absolutely crucial to what is going to happen on any particular day. If it is bright and sunny with a nice breeze, the chances are that the ball will not do very much but if there is cloud cover you can usually guarantee that it will move around.

REPUTATIONS

All grounds have certain reputations but, in recent years, none have been more notorious than LORD'S on the morning of a one-day final. Captains go there in fear of losing the toss, knowing from past experience that it can affect the outcome to a considerable degree. Not only in the NatWest Trophy Final, which starts at 10.30 on a September morning, but also in the Benson and Hedges Cup Final, which begins half an hour later in July, the pitch is often damp and there is a great advantage to be gained from batting second in spite of bad light later in the day. It is different in Test matches. In recent years, the pitches have still been a little damp at the start but you have more time to build an innings and if you can get through the first hour or two it should be good for batting for the next two days. After that, the pitch begins to crack and become uneven in bounce so it is not so good for batting last. It is a lucky captain who can put the opposition in to bat in a Lord's final but a brave one who does it in a Lord's Test.

You do not have to go far to find a complete contrast. Just across London at the OVAL, you know the pitch is almost certain to be dry, firm, fast and bouncy. It will stay like that throughout the match, whether it is a one-dayer or a five-day Test, and with little likelihood of turn, it is still generally a 'bat first' situation. I say 'generally' because as England discovered against South Africa in 1994 it can be at its fastest on the first day so if you are confident of bowling the other side out – or you are a little bit concerned about the opposition's attack, like four West Indian fast bowlers! – it can be a good idea to put them in.

Some pitches are much more difficult to assess, with HEADINGLEY a prime example. Apart from the weather conditions, much may depend on whether you are playing on one of the wickets which have been relaid in recent years or one of the older

David Gower – a record-breaking batsman, yet he was fooled by the Headingley pitch.

ones. The new wickets have been reasonably good for batting, unlike the older ones which would crack up and make the ball go up and down and seam around. But they remain unpredictable, as David Gower will testify. It led to his downfall as England captain in 1989 when he played four seamers, put Australia in and saw them score more than 600. They never looked back.

Generally speaking, the ball seams more in England than it does in other countries, mainly because there is more grass and dampness on the pitches, but there are other grounds around the world which are notorious for helping the seam. The GABBA at Brisbane used to be one of them until the start of the 1994–5 Ashes series when we came across a completely dry pitch perfect for Shane Warne, who destroyed us with eleven wickets in the match. Until then, Brisbane pitches had tended to be damp and green on the first morning and this, coupled with the steamy, sub-tropical atmosphere in Queensland, made it very conducive to both seam and swing bowling. By way of contrast, the WACA (Western Australia Cricket Association) ground in Perth is reckoned to be the hardest, fastest wicket in the world. It can be covered in huge cracks but they usually hold firm and the bounce remains true. The bowlers do get some respite from the Fremantle Doctor, the wind which blows across the pitch and can help the swing, but it is invariably a good batting wicket.

Richie Richardson – a law unto himself.

On the other side of the world, the QUEEN'S PARK OVAL in Trinidad is one of the hardest pitches to read. Like Brisbane, it is often damp and green on the first day but this is because the groundsman is trying to hide the fact that it will dry very quickly, start to crack and become uneven in bounce. I must admit that when we played the West Indies there in 1994 I didn't have a clue what to do if I won the toss. It didn't matter because Richie Richardson won it and decided to bat – which is not what I would have done given his attack. He was obviously banking on bowling last at us on a very up-and-down pitch and his decision was totally vindicated when we were all out for 46!

Elsewhere in the Caribbean, the pitches are not dissimilar to those in India and Pakistan which are not very good for swing and seam bowling and explain why they developed the idea of reverse-swing. Their hard, dry pitches and dusty outfields are a great help in scuffing the ball although there are certain grounds in England which can also assist the process. OLD TRAFFORD and the OVAL are fairly good in this respect, especially in a dry summer which leaves the outfields parched and rough.

When it comes to spin bowling, India is the place. The pitches there are pretty good for batting but they all turn from the second day. In fact the last time England were there they deteriorated to such an extent in BOMBAY and MADRAS that there were holes on a good length, which, needless to say, were very conducive to their spin trio of Kumble, Chauhan and Venkataparthy Raju.

GETTING IT RIGHT

While Test wickets may vary around the world, we have seen nothing in recent times to match the extraordinary fluctuation in the standard of pitches in county cricket. When I started playing for Lancashire in 1987 and for the next two years, we were using balls with huge, protruding seams on often under-prepared, grassy pitches. The combination produced a host of moderate seam bowlers plundering rich returns and left many good batsmen struggling for decent scores. Then, in 1990, we went to the other extreme. The seams were reduced, the pitches were ironed out into flat, lifeless strips and ordinary batsmen found themselves making double centuries while good bowlers were struggling to take wickets.

There has got to be a balance between the two to provide a fair contest between bat and ball and we are not going to get that by preparing wickets which resemble Test pitches. With eighteen first-class counties, there are simply not enough top-quality bowlers to go around so we cannot have pitches which offer them very little help. We must have pitches which have something in them for the bowlers but at the same time give good batsmen the chance to prosper. To this end, I would like to see groundsmen given a bit more freedom to experiment and use their skills instead of being restricted by some of the regulations we have had in recent years. One, stipulating that pitches had to be 'straw-coloured', was a failure. At grounds like Northampton and Derby, the pitches are so slow that there has to be some grass on them to enable the ball to carry through to the wicketkeeper and slips.

There are clear guidelines on what constitutes a 'fit' or 'unfit' pitch. Counties can now have twenty-five points deducted if they are adjudged to have prepared an 'unsuitable' pitch yet it seems to me that one is punished from time to time as a deterrent to the others while a lot of unsuitable pitches go unpunished.

TO COVER OR NOT TO COVER

One of the longest-running debates in county cricket, especially when two or three of the older players are gathered together, is on the question of whether pitches should be left uncovered, as they used to be, or covered, as they are now. Like many players, I played a lot of my early league cricket on uncovered pitches – in fact they were left uncovered, albeit with the bowlers' run-ups protected, during the day in my first county season – and I would not be against an experiment which saw us revert to playing on uncovered wickets. I believe it would bring greater variety to the first-class game and restore some of the skills that have been lost, in both batting and bowling. There is one snag which I discovered on discussing the subject with Ray Illingworth, who has a wealth of knowledge on these matters. It is that with the amount of loam and topsoil that has been put on pitches over the years, they are harder and faster than they used to be and could become very dangerous if they got wet on top and remained hard underneath. But if the groundsmen got rid of the loam and topsoil and went back to the 'natural' soil wickets of old, I think uncovered wickets could have a part to play in adding to the variety in English cricket.

66 Where's the groundsman's hut? If I had a rifle I'd shoot him now. 99

BILL O'REILLY, Australian leg-spinner, during England's 903 for 7 at the Oval in 1938

The Test and County Cricket Board's objective in its recommendations on the preparation of pitches suitable for first-class cricket reads:

'At the commencement of a match, the pitch should be completely firm, dry and true, providing pace and even bounce throughout, and should ideally wear sufficiently to give spinners some help later in the game.'

6 THE ROLLER

Rolling is not only an essential part of the preparation of any pitch but it is one way in which a captain can legitimately try to influence the conditions under which the match is being played.

Apart from the pre-match rolling, which in the case of a Test can start up to a month before the game, the captain of the batting side can ask for the pitch to be rolled for seven minutes before the start of each innings – other than the first innings – and before the start of each day's play. No other rolling takes place during the match.

Under the laws, the captain has a choice of the rollers available, which at a Test ground might range from a lightweight 8cwt. through a middleweight 18cwt. right up to a heavyweight 36cwt. or getting on for two tons. The top weight is mainly used in preparation, especially in English cricket where the Test and County Cricket Board recently introduced a regulation forbidding its use between innings on the grounds that it would take too much pace out of the pitch.

According to the TCCB's own guidelines on pitch preparation, rolling should begin with the light roller once all the surface water has disappeared. As the pitch dries, the weight of roller should be increased. Groundsmen should then use the heavy roller 'at every suitable opportunity' until all the moisture has gone.

At Old Trafford, for example, Lancashire's groundsman, Peter Marron, liked to use the heavy roller as much as he could and this resulted in some of the hardest pitches in the country, although he has recently decided not to give them quite so much rolling in order to get some 'give' in the surface.

For some groundsmen, rolling is a work of art in itself, particularly in Jamaica where the groundsman and a small army of helpers literally spin a huge manual roller all the way down the pitch to polish it and leave a shimmering, shiny surface. It is quite unbelievable because you can not only see your own reflection in it but the wicket's and the ball's as well.

CHOOSING THE RIGHT ONE

For the captain – the captain of the *batting* side, remember – the choice of roller is usually pretty straightforward. He will generally

Ducking Courtney Walsh on Sabina Park's shimmering pitch.

ask for the LIGHT roller if he is happy with the state of the pitch and does not want to change it too much.

He will also use the light roller if he is worried that the surface might be cracking up and he does not want to make it worse. He would certainly use a light roller on pitches like Lord's and Headingley which are prone to uneven bounce – as I did against the South Africans in 1994. And he would use the light roller if he was concerned that there might be moisture underneath because a heavy roller would bring it to the surface.

A captain will turn to the HEAVY roller if his side is batting on a quick wicket and he wants to take some of the pace out of it – which is what I did against South Africa at the Oval. It was a different story after the first two innings had been completed. We were clearly in the box seat by then so I asked for the light roller to keep the pace in the wicket for their second innings.

Ian Chappell was good enough to give me the benefit of his advice about the use of the roller in Australian conditions. He said that basically the wickets were so hard that a light roller made absolutely no difference to the surface. Generally the use of a heavy roller would give the batsmen a half-hour respite from the new ball so you should either use the heavy one or nothing at all.

Another occasion when the heavy roller will be trundled out is if you are in a strong position approaching the last innings and want to try to break the wicket up a bit by loosening any cracks there might be and thereby accentuating any uneven bounce.

That is the theory, anyway, but, as with everything else in cricket, you can never be sure it will work.

7 WINNING THE TOSS

66 When I win the toss on a good pitch, I bat. When I win the toss on a doubtful pitch, I think about it a bit and then I bat. When I win the toss on a very bad pitch, I think about it a bit longer and then I bat. 99

Thus spoke W. G. Grace and who am I to argue with him? Times have changed and so has the game of cricket but his advice is as sound today as it was in the last century. I had never put a side in to bat in a Test match until the second match of the 1994–5 Ashes series at Melbourne – and after Australia had won by 295 runs I was even more convinced that W. G. was right!

*Alec Stewart – vice-
captain and an expert
on pitches.*

As a general rule, Test match captains like to bat first, get a good score on the board and use it to put pressure on the opposition. It is never as easy batting second when you are facing a big total. If you are tempted to insert the opposition, you really have to be confident of bowling them out for 250 or fewer on the first day. Then you hope to take advantage of improved batting conditions on the second and third days, build up a big lead and put them under pressure in the second innings.

Most captains will take W. G.'s advice and bat first but Richie Richardson was a law unto himself in the West Indies in 1994 when we went through an amazing four-match sequence. In Jamaica, I won the toss and batted on what was a perfect batting pitch – yet he said he would have bowled; in Guyana, he won the toss on another perfect batting pitch and did bowl; in Trinidad, he won the toss and batted, when, given his attack, I would almost certainly have bowled; and in Barbados he won the toss again on a wonderful batting pitch and decided to bowl.

In one-day cricket, captains are much more flexible when it comes to the toss. Generally, you are looking to have the best of the batting conditions and, if the pitch looks good, I am a great believer in getting runs on the board and putting the other side under pressure to get them. If the pitch is damp, then you want to exploit that early on, which is why some teams have recently become almost paranoid about batting first in Lord's finals.

Another consideration is that some sides are particularly good at chasing targets and actually prefer to bat second. Lancashire, with lots of all-rounders in the middle-order, are particularly good at chasing and so was England's 1994 Texaco Trophy side because we had people like Phillip DeFreitas, Chris Lewis, Shaun Udal and Darren Gough, all bowlers who can bat.

In England, I would imagine that on many grounds sides prefer to bat second. On small grounds, such as Taunton, a reasonable target can be difficult to defend as the boundaries are well within range. Lancashire, batting second, would be confident of chasing anything up to eight or nine runs an over with wickets in hand.

It is different in Australia. On the huge grounds at Melbourne and Sydney, boundaries are much more difficult to come by and when we were there in 1994–5 we made a concerted effort never to let the asking rate rise above six an over. In those World Series matches, batting first proved to be the popular and effective option.

Much depends on what you consider to be your own particular strengths and weaknesses although you can still get it horribly wrong. My biggest blunder was on the Caribbean island of St Vincent where I was chatting to a guy on the dock of the bay the day before a one-day international. He told me I should bat first because when the tide came in late in the day batting became harder and I wish I had listened to him. Instead I took advice from Geoff Boycott and put the West Indies in. It was patently the wrong decision and we got hammered.

It is still not a bad thing to ask advice. People like Ray Illingworth, Keith Fletcher and, yes, Geoff Boycott have a lot of knowledge about wickets and, in the present side, my vice-captain, Alec Stewart, has a knack of getting most things right. But in the end it is your own decision and you should go with your gut feeling.

As for the toss itself, I don't have any superstitions, no one call I use all the time, no lucky coins. I normally ask the boys whether they think 'heads' or 'tails' might be lucky on the day. Phillip DeFreitas did give me a 50p piece which he said was a lucky coin before the first Test at Trent Bridge in 1994 and I used it throughout the New Zealand and South Africa series. Not that it did me much good. I lost the toss four times out of six!

There have been some funny moments, too. In the Caribbean, I went out to toss with the captain of the St Kitts and Nevis team and when he flipped the coin the wind blew it off the pitch. It had come down in my favour and I immediately said: 'We'll bat.' But he demanded a 're-toss' and I wasn't sure what the Laws of the Game said about such a situation. I could not think of anything that said the coin had to land on the wicket and fortunately one of our Press men was nearby with his *Wisden* handy and, having checked the Laws, we batted.

It was my turn to try it on when I went out with Ken Rutherford before a one-day international against New Zealand at Edgbaston. Up went the coin, Ken called correctly and said: 'We'll bowl.' At that point, a BBC cameraman intervened to say that the toss had not been carried out correctly, which, in his terms, meant that it had not been done at the right time for television. It looked a poor pitch to me and I was all for a re-toss but Ken would have none of it. In the end, we did a fake toss just for the TV cameras.

The toss, then, is important. It is something that you spend a lot of time thinking about before a game, even to the point of keeping the opposition waiting for another ten minutes after you have won it before you decide what to do. But it is crucial to remember – and to emphasise to your players – that the toss is not as important as the way you play. The toss may go for you or it may go against you but, in the final analysis, the better team usually wins.

❝ He could never make up his mind whether to call heads or tails. ❞

RAYMOND ILLINGWORTH on former England captain Colin Cowdrey

8 PACING THE GAME

Whatever form of cricket you are playing, it is important to have a game plan, a clear idea of what you are trying to achieve and how you are going to achieve it. From my point of view as a captain and opening batsman, my approach can be divided into two categories – building an innings in Test or county cricket, and setting or chasing targets in one-day cricket.

Test matches are not won by flashy fifties and sixties but by big hundreds, major innings, so every batsman, not just the openers, should be looking to bat for as long as possible. You want to be there for the best part of two days to put your side in a position of strength and exert maximum pressure on the opposition.

TAKING IT EASY As an opener, you should be looking to bat for four or five sessions and the way I set about it is by going in with a very positive attitude, believing that I am going to get a hundred every time. Cyril Washbrook, the great Lancashire and England batsman, told me a long time ago that people don't pay any attention to the fifties. It's the hundreds that make them sit up and take notice so I try to be very positive, both in defence and attack.

Naturally, the early part of the innings is the most difficult. You are not only facing the new ball but the bowlers are also at their freshest. They come running in with vigour and enthusiasm, the ball tends to swing more because it is new, it moves further off the pitch because the seam is at its most prominent and it bounces higher because it is hard. It also hurts more if it hits you. But there are things in your favour, too. The innings has just started so your concentration is acute, the adrenalin is flowing and these things can help you counter the advantages the bowlers have. Your first priority is to see off the new ball so that the more dashing batsmen, the strokeplayers, can come in when the ball is older, the bowlers are not so fresh and it is easier to make runs.

At the start, then, your nerves are on edge and your feet are not moving too well so I take it easy and try to play myself in. I am a fairly slow starter anyway so in the early stages I leave as many balls as possible and try to get off the strike as much as I can by taking quick singles and letting my partner take a fair share of the bowling. I look to get my feet moving, knowing that once I've batted for an hour or so I should be in a decent groove and ready to take things on. To help me do this, I set myself little targets which are relatively easy to achieve. I concentrate on getting to 10, then 20, then 30 and generally once you get past 40 or 50 you feel as though you are batting naturally and fluently.

Another thing I do is add two wickets, mentally, to the actual score. If we're cruising at 80 or 90 without loss on the first day of a Test match, I always bear in mind that if we do happen to lose a wicket, the next batsman could easily be out first ball. If you add those two wickets in your mind, it helps you to keep concentrating and not risk giving your wicket away. My concentration is generally good and I am very annoyed with myself if I get out to a poor shot. That does not happen too often because I try to play within my limitations and stick to the shots I know I can play well.

GETTING ON TOP

Some batsmen start their innings differently. Gehan Mendis, a very fine opening batsman for Sussex and Lancashire who could consider himself unfortunate not to have played for England, used to take another approach altogether. He would go in and try to smash the ball around from the start, getting on top of the bowling before settling down into a nice, steady rhythm of play.

Michael Slater, the fine opening batsman for New South Wales and Australia, is another very dominant player right from the start. Whereas I see the contest solely between myself and the ball, he sees it as a very personal one. He tries to intimidate and dominate the bowler psychologically and win the personal battle. At times it can be his downfall but if the bowlers are intimidated physically – and Viv Richards provided *the* classic example of this – it is a fair chance that they will bowl less aggressively at you.

I have never found that so easy to do but it is certainly the case that the major innings are always dominant ones. If you look at the biggest innings of recent times – Brian Lara's 375 for the West Indies against England in Antigua, his 501 for Warwickshire against Durham at Edgbaston – they have come when the batsman has been completely on top of the bowling.

Lara's approach, I read recently, is to play himself in for about an hour by which time he believes that he can score off every ball and take any bowler apart. He also sets himself targets – although his are a bit bigger than mine. He aims to get to his batting average (which, at the moment, stands at 60 in Tests and 58 in all first-class cricket) and

*Michael Slater –
dominant from the
start of an innings.*

then sets about improving on it. However you do it, whether you are
a Boycott or a Lara, it is imperative in first-class cricket for the
batsman to go on and on. Graham Gooch is always telling the
England batsmen, as, I believe, the late Kenny Barrington was always
telling him: 'Never give it away. The low scores, the noughts, can be
just around the corner so when you're in, you've got to make it count.'

I paid my dues very early in my Test career. In only my third Test match, I got 151 against New Zealand at Trent Bridge and could have gone on to a much bigger score. But it seemed a dead match which was always heading for a draw after rain on the first two days and I got myself out by hitting a lazy shot to mid-off. In my very next innings at Lord's, I was out for nought in Danny Morrison's first over. It taught me a very important lesson.

CHASING TARGETS

By its very nature, one-day cricket demands a different approach. But while games can be won by brilliant batting, the odd explosive 70 or 80, it is usually the more clinical, professional innings which settle the issue. This is what makes Lancashire's Neil Fairbrother probably the best one-day batsman in the world today. If you watch him play, if you study the way he goes about the business of winning matches from his position in the middle-order, you will see that it is all very cool and calculated. What he will try to do is force the fielders back by hitting the ball over their heads in the early stages of his innings and then, when he has got them back, he will simply pick up singles by manoeuvring the ball into the gaps.

Neil Fairbrother – probably the best one-day batsman in the world.

Being a steady sort of player, my role in the one-day games is to try to bat through the innings while the more dashing strokemakers play around me. Again, I look to break the task down into smaller targets. For example, in a Sunday League match, where a total of around 240 is reckoned to be a good score, I will set my sights on scoring about 110 of them. To my mind, the easiest way of doing that is to break it down into more achievable goals. So I look to have 20 after 10 overs, 50 after 25 overs, 85 after 30 overs and 110 by the end of the 40-over innings.

ARTIFICIAL

The one-day game is, of course, much more artificial than the genuine article and because of this different strategies are devised to cope with different regulations. In the 1992 World Cup, the restriction of having only two fielders outside a 25-metre circle in the first 15 overs of an innings led to Ian Botham opening the batting for England in the hope that he would be able to take advantage of the huge gaps in the outfield. In the event, the move was not as successful as New Zealand's tactic of using an off-spinner, Dipak Patel, to open the bowling and challenging the batsmen to hit him over the top.

Personally I am not in favour of all these restrictions, including the one which prevents fast bowlers from bowling any short-pitched balls above shoulder height. We had a situation in the World Series Cup in Australia in 1990 where Devon Malcolm bowled a superb, throat-high delivery to New Zealand's John Wright which flew off his glove to the wicketkeeper. John was on his way back to the pavilion when the umpire recalled him because he had called 'no-ball'. In my view, it was a perfectly legitimate dismissal and one example of why I am against artificial measures which make the game too biased towards the batsmen.

DECLARATIONS

There are times when a first-class match can go into a one-day mode and that is when one side declares and sets the other a target of a certain number of runs to win. If this gives both sides a chance of victory it is known as 'a sporting declaration' – although you do not get too many sporting declarations in Test matches.

Captains are generally pretty conservative when it comes to declaring in Tests because they are usually played over a series of three or five matches. In a five-match series, there is no need to make a risky declaration in its early stages because you hope to find yourselves in a winning situation later on; in a three-match series, you certainly don't want to risk losing the first one because it is always very difficult to pull it back once you have gone one-down.

I must admit that in my time as England captain there have not been too many occasions when I've been in a position to declare anyway. I was going to declare in only my second Test as captain against Australia at the Oval but we were all out before I had the chance. And I did declare against the West Indies in Barbados! But neither situation came into the 'sporting declaration' category. What I was trying to do on both occasions was to snuff them out of the game completely and demoralise them with the knowledge that they had no chance of winning. Happily it worked both times.

It was a different situation when I declared against South Africa in the second Test at Headingley in 1994. We were 1–0 down in a three-match series and I set them a target of more than 300 in only two sessions. It was a fairly cautious declaration, admittedly, but the thinking behind it was that the pitch was still playing well and the last thing we wanted was to lose and go into the final Test 2–0 down. If the pitch had been deteriorating, if the ball had been turning square or moving off the cracks, we may have been a bit more adventurous but Graeme Hick, Graham Thorpe and Alec Stewart had all made runs on it and there was no reason why the South Africans should not do the same. As it happened, the policy worked because the inevitable draw at Headingley was followed by victory at the Oval and a creditable drawn series.

My most controversial declaration came at Sydney in 1995 since it left Graeme Hick stranded on 98 not out and caused some consternation. It is never a nice position for a captain to be in and, in retrospect, I felt it was a mistake because, psychologically, we would have been much higher had I declared two runs later. As it was, perhaps the declaration flattened us a little.

The point is that I could have declared earlier or I could have declared later – but I declared when I did because I felt it was in the best interests of the side. I wanted two goes at Australia with the new ball and I felt we had messed around for two overs wasting what might have turned out to be valuable time. As I say, it might have been a mistake but, as captain, I only ever make decisions in good faith with the interests of the side in mind.

As a captain, you have to have the courage to make difficult decisions and the conviction to stand by them.

County games are not quite the same as Test matches because in the championship you are playing for points. You don't get any points for a draw so you have to try to win and therefore it's easier to gamble. County games also come round more often than Test matches and there is not quite the same intensity of feeling in victory or defeat. I am not saying that county players do not care as much but Test matches consist of two days' preparation and five days' cricket and the emotion of winning or losing is much greater.

CONTRIVED FINISHES

Declarations can produce the very best of cricket as both sides go for victory – and, sometimes, the very worst. This happened fairly frequently in the days of three-day cricket on exceptional batting pitches when neither side could bowl the other one out twice. But it still occurs in the best of circles when a team is desperate for victory and will deliberately give the other side runs to hasten a declaration or keep them interested in chasing a target.

The most blatant case I have been involved in was at Old Trafford in 1993 when Glamorgan, trying to make up for time lost to rain, presented Lancashire with 235 runs off 12 overs in half an hour. Our young fast bowler, Glen Chapple, scored a century off 27 balls in 21 minutes – the fastest ever recorded in first-class cricket – but he wasn't too proud of it. Matthew Maynard and Tony Cottey just tossed down a series of full tosses and long hops and Glen kept

FASTEST HUNDREDS
Genuine

Mins		
35	Percy Fender (Surrey v. Northants)	1920
40	Gilbert Jessop (Glos v. Yorks)	1897
40	Ahsan-ul-Haq (Muslims v. Sikhs)	1924
42	Gilbert Jessop (Southern Gents v. Players)	1907
43	Albert Hornby (Lancs v. Somerset)	1905

Contrived

21	Glen Chapple (Lancs v. Glamorgan)	1993
26	Tom Moody (Warwicks v. Glamorgan)	1990
35	Steve O'Shaughnessy (Lancs v. Leics)	1983
37	Chris Old (Yorks v. Warwicks)	1977
41	Nigel Popplewell (Somerset v. Glos)	1983

whacking them to the boundary where the fielders, standing just over the rope, would pick the ball up and throw it back. One fielder actually caught the ball behind the rope and signalled six. In the end, Glamorgan could say that the end justified the means because they won the match but it was an absolute farce.

The Reverend Andrew Wingfield-Digby, captaining Dorset, once gave Cheshire 56 runs in one over by instructing a bowler to send down fourteen consecutive wides, all of which went to the boundary, and Mark Harvey, playing for Lancashire's second team, went even further. He needed to give away 100 runs and did it by conceding 108 in one, unfinished over, bowling a succession of no-balls, costing two runs each, all of which went for four byes. There were eighteen deliveries, all of them no-balls, all of them worth six runs.

I can understand a captain's desire to do all that he can to achieve a result and especially in Lancashire where we seem to be frustrated by the weather more often than anybody, but those kind of situations are just ridiculous and cannot be within the spirit of the game.

THE SCIENCE OF BATTING

9 TAKING GUARD

When a player arrives at the crease, the first thing he does is to take guard from the umpire. It looks like a formality, just a quick check like straightening your tie before an interview, but it is much more important than that. Different batsmen take different guards and a lot of factors have to be taken into account.

First, a batsman's guard may be dependent on his height. Generally, he will want to have a guard so that when he takes up his stance and leans over his bat his head will be positioned over the off stump. A tall player, therefore, may take guard on leg stump because he has to lean further over his bat while a smaller player might take middle stump. Personally, I take middle-and-leg, although that is not altogether because of my height of six foot. There are other important reasons as well.

Much can depend on the relative strengths of your offside and legside play. If a batsman is missing out on balls outside his leg stump – that is, failing to score off deliveries that can often be considered as free hits – he may take a leg-stump guard to help him ease them through the legside. On the other hand, if a batsman finds that he is reaching or searching for the ball outside the off stump – 'fishing' as we call it – he may shift his guard over to middle.

A guard can also depend on a batsman's initial movement. Most of us have a 'trigger' move before we actually play the ball. Some batsmen will go back and across the crease, some will go forward and across, some go straight back, some go straight forward. Their guard will be determined by that first key movement.

My guard has evolved from my early days as a schoolboy and university cricketer when I used to take middle stump. I then found out that I was missing out on those legside deliveries so I shifted across to leg stump. That was how I stayed until I started playing first-class cricket when I discovered that I was getting out lbw far too often because I was not getting my front pad outside the line of the off stump. That is when I shifted to middle-and-leg, which was only a matter of an inch or so but sufficient to give me that happy medium between the two.

There are times when a batsman will take guard OUTSIDE or in front of the crease. When you are batting on a slow wicket without much bounce and the bowler is pitching the ball up and trying to get you out lbw, you may try to combat that by getting further forward. You hope that the square leg umpire will notice this and indicate your advanced position to the umpire at the bowler's end so that he can take it into consideration in any subsequent lbw appeal. Obviously the further the ball has to travel after hitting the pad, the less certain the umpire will be that it would hit the stumps.

Graham Gooch used to adopt this ploy when facing Australia's Terry Alderman – although it did not seem to alter the umpire's continually unfavourable judgment!

At other times, a batsman may take guard INSIDE the crease. If you are playing against a particularly quick bowler on a fast, bouncy wicket, you want to give yourself as much time as possible to see the ball and get into the correct position.

THE STANCE

Once the batsman has taken guard, he will probably adopt one of two basic stances. The first is the classical, 'closed' stance, where the batsman is sideways on with his feet comfortably balanced and his left shoulder pointing towards the bowler. The other is the 'open', two-eyed stance where the batsman is more chest-on towards the bowler.

I try to use the CLOSED stance most of the time, although sometimes I will have my left leg slightly withdrawn while remaining basically sideways-on. This is because my first movement tends to be slightly forward and across so if my left leg is somewhat removed from the sideways-on position, that first movement will not leave me playing across my front pad but alongside it.

I would employ the OPEN stance if I was facing a sustained barrage of fast bowling such as I have had to withstand against the West Indies. If you are too sideways-on, you can have a blind spot which makes the short ball, especially the bouncer, difficult to detect.

This happened to me in Jamaica in 1994 when Courtney Walsh produced a sustained spell of hostile bowling. Before I finally succumbed, I felt ill at ease precisely because I was too sideways-on and therefore having trouble with balls aimed at the ribs. Subsequently on that tour, I opened up my stance, with better results.

(BELOW, LEFT)*Tony Greig holds the bat high while* (RIGHT) *Viv Richards adopts a more comfortable stance.*

Graeme Hick used to employ the UPRIGHT stance with the bat held high above the ground which was first introduced by Tony Greig and taken up by a lot of English batsman. It is not so common these days although Graham Gooch still uses it because the top half of his body is quite heavy so that when he crouches over his bat he tends to take his bodyweight towards the offside. This can make him lose his balance and fall over as he did when Australia's Terry Alderman kept getting him out lbw in 1989. Graham therefore still prefers the upright stance which keeps his bodyweight balanced and helps him to go backwards and forwards rather than across his stumps. Graeme Hick, on the other hand, has discarded it and changed to a more classical stance, leaning over with his bat on the ground and playing with a fluid, up-and-down motion. It is a more natural and comfortable position and he looks all the better for it.

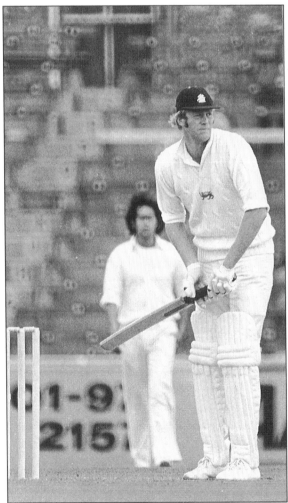

10   THE SHOTS

Forward defensive

Played to a straight ball of full length which you are trying to keep out of your stumps. You push the left pad forwards towards the pitch of the ball, bring the bat down straight and play the ball alongside the pad into the ground. You do not grip the bat too hard but use what we call 'soft hands' so that any deflection off the bat and pad will not carry to the close catchers.

Forward defensive – Geoff Boycott uses soft hands to keep the ball away from the close catchers.

Backward defensive

Played to a straight ball of shorter length to which you cannot play forward. You take your right foot back parallel to the crease, keep your left elbow high and play sideways-on to the bowler with an

Backward defensive with the left elbow high.

angled bat. Again use soft hands so that any nicks do not carry to the fielders.

On drive

Played to a half volley or a ball of fuller length on middle or middle-and-leg which you are looking to dispatch past the bowler between the stumps and mid-on. It is a particularly pleasing shot, played especially well by Australia's Michael Slater, which all the best batsmen play because they know they are hitting the ball in the right area – the 'V' as we call it between mid-on and mid-off – and it is completely safe. You push the left pad towards the pitch of the ball, inside the line, bring the bat down straight and follow through with your head over the ball so that it stays down.

Off drive

Another classical stroke which is again played to a full or near half volley but this time to a ball which is more towards the off stump. It is another safe shot because you are hitting in the 'V' between the stumps and mid-off. Again you push your left pad towards the pitch of the ball, bring the bat down straight and follow through with your head over the ball. While your left (or top) hand and left elbow are high and doing all the work, it is your right (or bottom) hand which puts the power into the drive.

*Cover drive – a
classical stroke.
Boycott.*

Cover drive

Exactly the same, technically, as the off drive except that it is played
to a ball which is a little bit wide of the off stump and you are
looking to hit it between mid-off and cover – in other words,
through extra cover. If the ball is even wider, you will look to hit it
between cover and point, in which case the shot is more of a **square
drive**.

Cut

Played to a ball which is short and wide enough of the off stump to
give you room to play an attacking shot. You have defended the
short, straight ball with a backward defensive shot, you have wisely
left alone the short ball which is only just wide of the off stump, but

now there is enough width to go on the offensive. Pick the bat up high, take your right leg across so that your head is over the line of the ball and bring the bat down to hit it between gully and point. It is important to roll the wrists to keep the ball down – which is why you must also remember to lift the bat high. If you do not lift it high enough, it is almost impossible to play the cut – or the pull and the hook, for that matter – and keep the ball down.

Pull

Played to a short ball which is too straight to leave alone and not wide enough to attempt to cut. You move your right leg backwards followed by your left so that you are square-on to the bowler and you hit the ball from almost in front of your eyes, again with a roll of

Pulling with a roll of the wrists to keep the ball down.

the wrists to keep it down. The height is such that if you miss the shot, the ball will hit you in the chest.

Hook

Played to an even shorter delivery, a bouncer which lifts above shoulder-height. You move inside the line of the ball by going over towards the off stump before hooking it, again with a roll of the wrists, down towards deep backward square leg or fine leg. If you miss it, the ball should go past your left ear – with a bit of luck. Should the ball be outside the off stump, you can hook it in front of square, provided you can get into position quickly enough. In this case, you are playing the shot from outside the line, so if you miss it, the ball should go past your right ear. This is a much more risky shot

Keeping the head over the ball.

because you have less control and it is not to be recommended unless you are well into your innings and seeing the ball well.

Glance

This is a bread-and-butter shot, a get-off-the-mark shot for any self-respecting batsman. It is played to a ball which is around middle-and-leg or drifting down the legside. It can be played on the front foot, if the ball is far enough up, or the back foot, if it is short. You should get slightly outside the line of the ball and just turn your wrists and send it on its way down to fine leg for an easy single – or more.

Sweep

Played against a spin bowler, particularly an off-spinner but also a leg-spinner or a slow left armer, if the ball is pitching outside leg stump. It is played to a ball of normal length and you take a big stride forward, get down on your right knee and hit it with a horizontal bat, once again rolling the wrists to keep the ball down. Batsmen without too much confidence in the sweep will only play it if the line is right, on or just outside leg stump; the best exponents, like Graham Gooch, will sweep on length. He gave a classic demonstration during the 1987 World Cup when he swept the Indian spinners to oblivion, hitting them wherever he wanted, fine, square or in front of square, with shots of bludgeoning power or fine precision.

Reverse sweep

Predominantly a one-day shot, usually played against an off-spinner when he is bowling on middle or middle-and-leg with a packed legside field. To score runs quickly, a batsman will either back away and try to smash the ball through the offside or he will revert to the reverse sweep – or in Darren Gough's case, the reverse pull! You put your left leg forward but, instead of sweeping the ball to fine leg, you turn the bat round so that the face is pointing towards cover and sweep the ball towards third man. It can be a very destructive shot because it is very annoying, frustrating and unsettling for the bowler, but, as Mike Gatting discovered during the World Cup Final in Calcutta, it can be very self-destructive, too. The pundits are very unforgiving if you get it wrong.

Pick-up

Another bread-and-butter shot for any batsman worth his salt. It is played to a ball of full length on leg stump which you are aiming to deposit over midwicket or square leg. It is simply a matter of judging the length and picking the ball up off your hips with a straight or slightly slanted bat, depending on where you want to hit it. All good batsmen are strong on their legs and see this shot as a free hit. Would that there were more.

Graham Gooch – all good batsmen are strong on the leg side.

11   THE BATTING ORDER

There are many things to be considered in deciding on the batting order, quite apart from the relative abilities of the batsmen in the side. These include their personal preferences and where they feel most comfortable, their temperaments and how they will react to particular situations, and their special skills and how they can be best utilised for the good of the team.

For a start, you look for two openers who are not necessarily the best players in the side but should certainly have the best technique to deal with the new ball. Naturally, you want them to bat for as long as possible but their main job is to lay a foundation or, at least, provide some protection for the quicker scorers, the strokeplayers, in the middle-order. In this way, you hope they will be able to go in when the ball is older, the bowlers are not so fresh and they can play more positively.

The differences between the middle-order batsmen can be fairly intangible. They ought to be able to bat anywhere from number three to number six but you have to remember that at five and six they may have to contend with the second new ball, certainly in a Test match. It is useful, therefore, to have batsmen in those positions who are used to dealing with it.

The question of how best to use the undeniable talent among England's middle-order batsmen is one of the problems that has faced the selectors during my time as captain. Where, for example, should players like Graeme Hick, Robin Smith, Graham Thorpe and Mark Ramprakash bat if we are going to get the best possible value out of them, bearing in mind that they all go in at numbers three or four in their county sides?

One of the factors that I had not really appreciated until he mentioned it to me is that Graeme Hick prefers to bat at number three because it means he is able to dictate the situation.

If he goes in at 10 for 1 or 20 for 1, the match situation has not yet been established and he can set the terms and dictate the game. If he is batting at number five and finds himself going in at 20 for 3, the match situation has already been established and he feels that he is forced to be more defensive and cannot play his natural game. Similarly, if he goes in at 300 for 3, the situation has again been set for him and he is not able to dictate the terms in the way that he likes.

Graeme's problems stemmed from the start of his Test career when he was picked in his favourite position and hailed as the answer to England's problems at number three. But, for one reason or another, he did not get enough runs to maintain the position and soon found himself being shunted up and down the order. Now, after one or two technical adjustments which have helped to restore his confidence, we have reverted to picking him at number three where he gets in early and plays his natural game. He has been much more successful of late and I would think this will be his role in the England side for the foreseeable future.

Graeme Hick – likes to dictate the situation.

Generally speaking, number three is not a position for younger players, or those just starting their Test careers. It is better to pick them at number five or number six where it is a little bit easier to bed them in. If you look at the West Indies, they blooded the nineteen-year-old Shivnarine Chanderpaul at number six against England, and Australia introduced Michael Bevan, a prolific scorer in Sheffield Shield cricket, in the same position against Pakistan. England did the same thing with Mark Ramprakash when he was brought in, with some success, against the West Indies in 1991 and I probably made a mistake in thrusting John Crawley into the number three spot on his debut against South Africa in 1994. We quickly rectified that by settling him in at number six.

There does come a stage, however, when the younger players are not so young any more and when we went to the West Indies in 1994 I felt that the time had come for the likes of Ramprakash and Nasser Hussain to show us what they were made of, to prove that they were not novices any more. They had enough experience, not necessarily in terms of Test cricket but certainly in terms of first-class cricket, and were good enough players, I felt, to cope with the extra responsibility.

Ready for more responsibility - (BELOW LEFT) *Mark Ramprakash and* (RIGHT)*Nasser Hussain.*

The whole thrust of that tour was that I felt the Gower, Lamb, Gatting, Gooch era was coming to a close and young players had to take us forward. The likes of Mark Ramprakash and Nasser Hussain were no longer first-time tourists but tough and reasonably experienced cricketers who were strong enough mentally and wanted it badly enough to succeed in the hard school of Test cricket. That is why we put Ramprakash in at number three. I believed then

and I still believe now that he has the ability to make a success of that position although, in the event, he did not do so.

Some people thought that I should have given the job to Robin Smith but I felt he was a key player on that tour and that to let him bat where he himself felt happiest was the right thing to do. Maybe, in retrospect, I was wrong. Maybe Robin should have gone in at number three. Then again, maybe Graeme Hick should have been there. But, in my opinion, they were our best two players and I wanted them at numbers four and five. In Robin's case, he had expressed a desire to bat at four and I was looking to give him plenty of responsibility in what is a pivotal position and hoping that he would respond to that responsibility. Sadly it did not really happen until the final Test in Antigua – and by then Brian Lara had batted us out of the game.

A further complication arises when you have a left-hander like Graham Thorpe in the side. He could count himself unlucky to be left out of the 1994 series against New Zealand when we had a policy of playing five specialist batsmen plus an all-rounder in Craig White. But when he was recalled against South Africa he presented the selectors with a problem because we then had six batsmen, four of whom – Graham Gooch, Alec Stewart, Graeme Hick and myself – wanted to bat in the top three.

Even if we had accommodated them all in the first four, it would have left Graham Thorpe batting at number five – and we wanted the left-hander to come in earlier to break up the right-handers and upset the rhythm of the South African bowlers. After much deliberation, we decided that Graham Gooch should revert to his favourite role of opener and Alec had to make the sacrifice and drop to number five, with Graeme Hick at three, Graham Thorpe at four and John Crawley at six.

By the time we went to Australia a couple of months later we had a different formation in mind. There, the original plan was for Alec Stewart to go back to opening the innings with Graham Gooch batting at number five – although we had to think again when Alec broke a finger before the opening match, and did it again in the second Test

The consideration there was that Graham Gooch is a particularly fine player of spin bowling who had dealt with Shane Warne's leg breaks and googlies better than anyone when we first saw him in England in 1993. We also felt that in view of Graham's advancing years – he was forty-one after all – and the Australian climate he would probably find it easier going in down the order after a long, hot day in the field.

In any case, numbers five and six are critical positions in Test match cricket. It is important to get off to a good start but if you can consolidate that by having people who can come in later on and score big hundreds like Steve Waugh has done for Australia it makes an enormous difference. Most recently, it has been where England have struggled most. Generally, we have had good starts, only to become unstuck in the middle order.

12 BATTING PARTNERS

There have been some great opening partnerships over the years – names like Hobbs and Sutcliffe, Hutton and Washbrook, Simpson and Lawry, Edrich and Boycott rolling off the tongue like fish and chips or roast beef and Yorkshire pudding.

In my time, Gordon Greenidge and Desmond Haynes were as good as any I have seen although Australia have been well served by Geoff Marsh and either David Boon or Mark Taylor. And I like to think that Graham Gooch and Mike Atherton came into the category of decent opening pairs.

Such liaisons are not just about two good players coming together by accident and producing a string of decent stands. They are also about how the partnerships work, how the batsmen complement each other, how they communicate and, essentially, how they run between the wickets. A right-hand / left-hand combination like Bobby Simpson and Bill Lawry and John Edrich and Geoff Boycott can be very effective. So can contrasting styles like the adventurous Greenidge and the more cautious Haynes, who were the most enduring partners of them all, and – dare I say? – Gooch and Atherton.

I always felt that there was the basis of a good partnership between Graham and myself because we complemented each other pretty well. He is a very strong, aggressive player, a fast scorer who hits a lot of boundaries. In contrast, I like to play myself in, getting off the strike as much as I can by running plenty of singles. Consequently our running between the wickets was crucial and we had hardly any mix-ups or misunderstandings along the way.

Partners –
(RIGHT) *Hobbs and Sutcliffe*

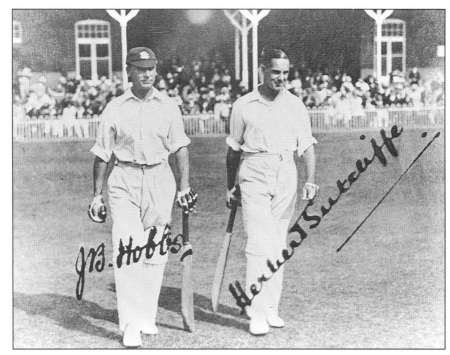

(BELOW LEFT)
Greenidge and Haynes
(RIGHT) *Gooch and Atherton.*

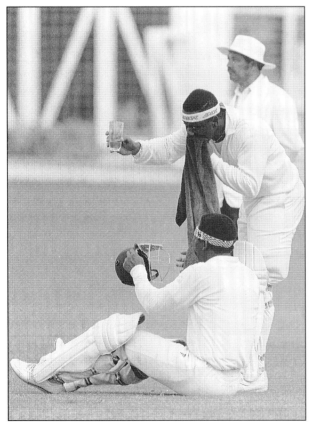

TALKING ...

Talking to each other is very important. When you go out to bat with a senior partner, you can learn an awful lot about batting in general and Test match cricket in particular by talking to him, and, more to the point, listening to what he has to say.

I have received most of my batting education from 'Goochy'. You can have all the coaching in the world and spend as much time as you like practising in the nets but it is out in the middle that you ply your trade. I have learned an enormous amount by batting at the other end from a bloke who, under all conditions and against all types of bowling, has been as good as any batsman of his time.

Not that he is one of the game's great talkers. If you are going well, he will give you little words of encouragement like 'Looking good' or 'Keep it going.' And, whatever the situation, he never stops reminding you: 'Don't give it away.'

There are times when you might be struggling against a particular bowler and will want a serious chat about your game plan. This happened when we were playing Australia in 1993 and Graham and I were two of the England batsmen who did have some success against Shane Warne – he more so than me. I remember us talking about where we were going to score off Warne, how we were going to play him when he went round the wicket and that kind of thing.

But that only happens when you are facing an especially tricky situation and you feel the need to work out an answer to it. More often than not, when you see two batsmen chatting in the middle of the pitch, they will be talking about anything but cricket. And this will almost certainly be the case if Robin Smith is one of them. He likes to talk and keep up a line of communication with his partner but he will do it with jokes or, perhaps, a few suggestions about where we might go for a drink or a meal afterwards. It is part of his approach to batting. He tries to lift himself by being very positive, buoyant and almost brash out in the middle and does not want a lot of serious, technical stuff about cricket. He wants to enjoy himself and feel good about his game.

RUNNING ...

Running between the wickets is obviously the key to a good partnership. The basic ground rules are very simple. If the ball is in front of square, the striker will call. If the ball is behind square, the non-striker will call.

It is the ball that is hit square of the wicket, towards point or square leg, that is a bit dodgy. I tend to leave those calls to the striker, who is in the best position to see the line of the ball, and trust his judgment.

TRUST is the most important thing in a partnership. If you can trust the other bloke with your wicket in his hands and respond to his call, then you will usually get home safely. It is when there is hesitation through lack of trust that the problems occur.

Some batsmen are just not very good runners of singles. Strong, fast-scoring players like Robin Smith and Graeme Hick are boundary-hitters and because that is the way they get most of their runs they are not so alert to the singles. Others, like Steve Rhodes, like to knock the ball around and keep the scoreboard ticking over with singles.

Steve is a great singles runner. I have a vivid memory of a Test match against New Zealand when I had batted for a while with Robin Smith and the scoring had become completely stagnant. I was struggling, totally out of form and just holding up one end, when Steve came in and immediately started tapping and running and the scoreboard was moving again.

Quick singles upset the fielding side and are crucial to batting success, partly because they keep the score moving, partly because they disrupt the bowlers' rhythm. A bowler likes to have six consecutive balls at one batsman and there is nothing he likes less than to bowl six good balls and find that he has still conceded two or three singles in the over. It is frustrating for both him and his fielders – which is why in the England team we stress the need to keep looking for singles.

The best partners do not actually say very much when they are running between the wickets. When you get to know somebody very well, when you trust him, it only requires a look to tell you to run. I have best had this kind of telepathy, which can only come from having one particular partner for a period of time, with three batsmen. I had it with Graham Gooch when we were opening together, with Alec Stewart when we were partners all through the 1994 West Indies tour, and with Neil Fairbrother when I was batting at number three for Lancashire and he was at number four.

WATCHING ...

To sum up, good partners need an eye for a single, a simple calling system, trust and a complete understanding of what the other is going to do. They have to be quick and athletic to get to the other end when they are called for those sharp singles and they need a working knowledge of the opposition fielders, which ones are good and which ones are not so good. You would not take too many singles to South Africa's Jonty Rhodes, for example. You also need to know whether fielders are right-handed or left-handed. I was once

playing for the MCC against Yorkshire at the Scarborough Festival
and after making a hundred in the first innings I was looking good
in the second. I had scored 20 or more when my partner, John Carr,
called me for a quick single to Phil Robinson's left hand. What John
had forgotten was that although Phil is a right-hand batsman he
throws with his left hand and I was run out by a direct hit on the
stumps.

EMBARRASSING Having told you all about running between the wickets, I have to
admit that I have been involved in some shocking run-outs in my
time, the worst of them costing me dearly against Australia at Lord's
in 1993. I was on 97 when I clipped Allan Border to the midwicket
boundary. I had completed two as Merv Hughes ran round to cut
the ball off and I called my partner, Mike Gatting, for a third. I was
on my way when Mike sent me back and, as I turned, I slipped on
the green grass at the edge of the pitch. Merv hurled the ball down
the hill, wicketkeeper Ian Healy gathered it well and I was run out
by yards as I tried to crawl back on my knees.

Another embarrassment, heightened by the media-invented
rivalry between Alec Stewart and myself for the England captaincy,
came in a Test match against India at Bombay. It was a classic mix-
up. There were mitigating circumstances in that I had only just got
back into the England side, which meant that we had not batted
together very often, and Bombay's Wankhede Stadium is a very
noisy place to play cricket. So when Alec pushed the ball into the
covers and called for a quick single, he did not hear my immediate
shout of 'No' and kept on running. What is more, he was watching
the line of the ball and it was not until he reached the non-striker's
end that he looked up and realised I was still there!

We finished up charging for the same end where there was a
delay of what seemed ages before the umpire gave Alec out. To
make matters worse, the Press misinterpreted the situation as me
standing my ground because I had lost the vice-captaincy to Alec
while I had been out of the side through injury. The truth is that it
was just a simple mistake. We were both at fault: Alec for ball-
watching and me for not trusting his call.

There have been other running disasters when I have been playing
for England, including one involving Neil Fairbrother and Chris
Lewis which illustrated the dangers of batting with somebody who is
extremely quick between the wickets. Neil is no slouch himself but
on that occasion in Sri Lanka Chris was too quick for him. Neil was
also involved in a disastrous run-out against Zimbabwe at Brisbane

❝ Hobbs and Sutcliffe were the perfect opening partners. They could play on all types of wickets and were excellent judges of a run. ❞

SIR LEN HUTTON

in the 1994–5 World Series tournament. Cantering for an easy single, he got the shock of his life when a direct hit, confirmed by the third umpire, brought about his downfall. It hopefully taught him the dangers of jogging easy singles, when you ought to be pushing hard for every run in one-day cricket.

Then there was the tragic case of Mark Ramprakash which contributed to our collapse to 46 all out when we needed only 195 to beat the West Indies in Trinidad. I had been out first ball and Mark turned his first delivery to fine leg to get off the mark. It was a comfortable single but he had developed a habit of turning and sliding a couple of yards before deciding whether to go for a second. In this instance, the bowler, who had followed through, was obscuring his vision but he set off, Alec Stewart set off from the other end, Mark hesitated, Alec hesitated – and, as ever, hesitation was fatal.

IN PARTNERSHIP

	Tests	Avge	100s
Hobbs and Sutcliffe (England)	25	87·81	15
Gooch and Atherton (England)	24	65·55	7
Hobbs and Rhodes (England)	36	61·31	8
Hutton and Washbrook (England)	28	60·00	8
Simpson and Lawry (Australia)	34	59·93	9
Gavaskar and Chauhan (India)	36	53·75	10
Edrich and Boycott (England)	21	52·25	6
Greenidge and Haynes (West Indies)	89	47·32	16
Marsh and Taylor (Australia)	21	46·83	4
Boon and Marsh (Australia)	24	46·77	5

(Qualification: over 20 Tests)

*Records up to the end of the 1994 season

13 ALL IN THE MIND

Batting is about a lot of things – technique, confidence, courage, concentration, talent and temperament. But the greatest of these is temperament

A genius like Brian Lara, who is blessed with all those qualities, is always going to be a great player. But what often separates those of equal gifts, what divides those who make the grade and those who do not, what determines how you are able to cope with the game of cricket, depends on those six inches between your ears.

Temperament is not something that can be taught. It is not to be found in the coaching manuals. Unless you are born with it, it only comes with experience. Graham Gooch, who began his Test career with a 'pair' and was dropped after only two matches before developing into one of England's greatest players, admits that the mental side of the game is something he never mastered until he was in his late thirties.

If you look at the preparation that players go through before the start of a season or before going away on tour, it is incredibly thorough. There are the fitness programmes, the technical work, the hours of practice in the nets and out in the middle. Yet very little attention is paid to the psychology of the game. For a brief period, England did have a sports psychologist called Peter Terry but I am convinced that this aspect of the game should be done on a one-to-one basis rather than as a team.

VISUALISATION

For a batsman, mental preparation is absolutely vital. You have to know what type of bowlers you are going to be up against. And if it is a particularly high-class bowler like Curtly Ambrose you have to remember the times when you have made runs against him. You must have positive thoughts, visualise the success you have had against him in the past and visualise the success you are going to have against him this time.

To this end, I have videotapes of the times when I was feeling particularly good and batting particularly well. At the moment, the tape I have with me records the 144 I made against the West Indies – Curtly and all – in the second Test in Guyana in 1994.

Curtly Ambrose –
remember the good
times, if you can!

Other players will carry tapes which remind them of the times when they were playing really badly so that they can study their faults and learn from their mistakes. But I think it is just as important, if not more so, to have on record those occasions when you were feeling great, everything was working smoothly and you just knew you were going to get runs. Seeing an innings like that on video when you are struggling and out of form can jog your memory and get you back into the rhythm of playing well.

If you go out to bat with negative thoughts, if you think you are going to get out cheaply, then, inevitably, you will. I remember opening the batting with Mark Lathwell when we were facing a massive Australian score of 653 for 4 declared in only his second Test at Headingley in 1993. He was a bit overawed by the occasion and struggling to come to terms with playing for England.

As we walked out to a standing ovation, I said: 'This is how they'll be when you come back with a hundred to your name.'

To which Mark replied: 'But this is not how they'll be if you get nought.'

It suggested to me that his frame of mind was not entirely positive and, perhaps, not as it should have been. And he did get nought.

KEY THOUGHTS

Batsmen have different ways of getting themselves into the right frame of mind before they go in. Graham Gooch will have his earphones on, listening to 'Land of Hope and Glory' or something equally stirring. I like to bat in my England sweater, showing the three lions to the bowler. It's little things like these that spur you on.

At the start of their innings, batsmen will also have key thoughts. All sorts of things are buzzing around in your mind, the crowd is cheering and the adrenalin flowing, but as the bowler runs in you have to blank everything out and concentrate on what for you is the one thing that matters above all else. For me, it is to watch the ball so I keep telling myself over and over again, 'Watch the ball, watch the ball,' and focus all my attention on it.

It is always important but especially so if you are facing a fast bowler like Merv Hughes who will be spitting and snarling and looking as mean and nasty as he possibly can. At times like that, it is a great help if you can avoid looking at his face and just watch the ball all the way.

SELF-DOUBT

There will be periods either at the start of an innings or some time during it when you know you are struggling, your feet are not moving, your hands don't feel right and you think you are completely out of form. It is your mental preparation coupled with your experience which will help you through these moments of anguish and self-doubt.

Before the 1991 Sydney Test against Australia, when I eventually made 105, I felt desperately out of touch, having scored few runs in the previous Tests and state games. Basically, when you are so out of form, everything feels out of rhythm. Instead of watching the ball, you are thinking of your backlift, your head and everything else. Two things worked for me in that innings. The first was blocking out all the negative thoughts and concentrating solely on the ball; the second was using a kind of self-kidology, convincing myself that I had just come off the back of a big hundred the previous match.

Again, some batsmen do it differently and try to blast their way out of trouble. But I just try to occupy the crease, concentrating on staying there and not worrying about scoring runs, in the knowledge that they will come eventually. Sometimes you just have to be bloody-minded about it and say to yourself: 'This bloke is *not* going to get me out at all costs.'

I took this attitude against South Africa at Headingley in 1994. I had been engulfed in controversy following that so-called 'ball-tampering' episode at Lord's, I had not had a county game for two weeks and for the first hour I was just batting from memory. Gradually things began to come together and I went on to score 99 – and it was all down to my own bloody-mindedness in saying: 'No way are these guys going to get me out.' It was much the same against South Africa in 1995–6 when I batted nearly 11 hours to make sure we saved the Second Test at Johannesburg.

DON'T BE DAFT

There are other times when you feel bang in form and on top of the world – and then you have to concentrate even harder, telling yourself not to get carried away and do something silly. When Alec Stewart scored his two hundreds in the Barbados Test against the West Indies, I was actually scoring quicker than he was in the first innings. I was really flowing and feeling great. I had reached 85 when I got myself out with a dreadful shot and it was all because I was feeling so good that I thought I could hit every ball for four.

I will remember that and it will remind me that no matter how well things seem to be going I must not lose my concentration and do anything daft.

GAME PLAN

What made it particularly galling was that, whatever faults I may have, giving my wicket away is not usually one of them. I have a feeling that some batsmen do not know how they are going to play, how aggressive they are going to be – and how defensive. One thing I can say is that over the years I have come to know my own game. I know my shots, I know my limitations and I stick by them. Most of the time.

You *must* have a plan for different conditions and different bowlers. Against a quick bowler on a bouncy wicket, I will keep telling myself to be careful with one of my favourite shots, which is the back-foot drive. This is because the extra pace and bounce can get you into trouble with it. Similarly, against an off-spinner on a

Shane Warne – no ready answer.

turning wicket, you should steel yourself not to try to hit him through the offside, unless you get a full half volley. You should settle for hitting with the spin, through mid-on or midwicket and behind square with the sweep.

Before we went to Australia in 1994, people were always asking us: 'How are you going to play Shane Warne?' There was no ready answer, no way you could instruct every batsman to play him in a certain way. Each individual had to work it out for himself and the key to that was to get to know his line of approach and his variations. It was going to be no good having to face him thinking to yourself: 'Blimey, where am I going to get my runs against this guy?' You had to be prepared so that you knew how you were looking to play him and where you were looking to score.

Salim Malik obviously had the answer during Australia's visit to Pakistan in 1994 when he averaged over 100. First, he was able to pick Warne's variations – and that helps. Second, he shifted his guard over to leg stump and effectively decided to hit Warne through the offside despite his predominantly leg-stump line.

This is the mental side of batting which must be allied to your technical and natural ability. It is part of the learning curve and it can take years to make you into a better player.

THE BOWLING ARTS

14 STYLES AND TECHNIQUES

If batting is a science, which is a pursuit of 'systematic and formulated knowledge' according to one dictionary, then bowling is an art, an 'imitative or imaginative' exercise of skill. I know you can have batting artists like David Gower, who could cover the canvas with the most delicate of strokes, and scientific bowlers such as Dennis Lillee, who explored all the angles in his search for wickets. But for sheer imagery in cricket, you have to look to the great bowlers and the way they exercise their skill to exploit the prevailing conditions.

SWING

Let us start with the swing bowlers. I have already outlined the weather conditions which are most likely to help the ball to swing but there are other factors involved as well. First, there is the bowler's action, which basically needs to be sideways-on for out-swing and more open-chested for in-swing. Second, there is the position of the wrist, which needs to be cocked and behind the ball. And third, there is the condition of the ball, which, in my opinion, is the main reason why there are not so many swing bowlers around as there used to be.

To bowl OUT-SWING – in other words to make the ball move in the air away from the right-hand batsman towards the slips – you hold the ball with the first two fingers either side of the seam pointing towards the slips or third man. You use a classical, sideways action with your left shoulder towards the batsman and your head looking over it. The ball is then delivered with the wrist behind it and firmly cocked as you push the ball towards first slip.

This is the traditional, time-honoured way of doing it although these days you do see a lot of very successful bowlers bowling out-swing with a chest-on action. Two of the great West Indian bowlers, Curtly Ambrose and Malcolm Marshall, as well as Phil Newport, who

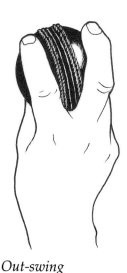

Out-swing

In-swing

Waqar Younis – the greater the pace, the greater the reverse swing.

is one of the biggest out-swingers in English cricket, can all do this, which leads me to believe that the key factor must be the wrist action.

For IN-SWING – that is moving the ball into the right-hander towards fine leg – the grip is reversed so that the seam is pointing towards fine leg. The action is much more open so that the chest is pointing towards the batsman and you are looking inside your left shoulder. As the ball is delivered, the wrist breaks and pushes it towards leg slip.

With REVERSE-SWING, everything seems to happen in reverse as the term implies – and, unlike normal swing, the greater the pace, the more the reverse-swing. You do not find too many medium-pacers making the ball reverse-swing to any great extent. It is the genuine quick bowlers like Wasim Akram, Waqar Younis and Darren Gough who are the great exponents.

Reverse-swing is usually towards the batsman, the ball ducking into him at the last moment. Reverse-swingers rarely get the ball to swing away but they do turn it round so that it just holds its own. And at their pace, with the batsman looking for the big in-ducker, getting the ball to hold its own is usually enough.

A mystery

As I have said, this is a relatively new technique developed in dry and dusty conditions where the ball soon becomes worn and scuffed – but it has quickly caught on everywhere because balls simply do not seem to swing in the old-fashioned way as much as they used to do.

Ian Botham once told me that when he started playing first-class cricket the ball would *always* swing. Sometimes he would hold it for an out-swinger and it would swing in – so he would just turn the ball round and it would swing out.

That is definitely not the case these days. For some reason the Australian Kookaburra balls tend to swing more than their English counterparts when new, but generally speaking none of them swing like they used to do. Take, for example, Wasim Akram, a superb exponent of swinging the old ball. To swing the old ball both ways as he does shows he has a superb wrist action. Yet, it is rarely that he swings a new ball.

I can remember Alec Bedser telling me that in his day if a young bowler went to the Surrey nets for a trial and could not swing the new ball he would be turfed out immediately and not invited back. Yet I have seen South Africa's Fanie de Villiers, who can swing the ball as much as anybody in the game these days, find that he sometimes cannot swing it at all. I do not know why, but I am convinced that this is because the balls are not the same as they used to be.

❝ Cricket balls are very fickle things. I suspect it is possible for quite subtle things to be done to them with quite dramatic effects. ❞

ANDREW LEWIS, Lecturer at University of Hertfordshire

Early or late?

Finally there is the question of what makes the ball swing EARLY or LATE. Much depends on the bowler's arm action. If he has a low, slingy action – like Lancashire's Peter Martin – he will deliver the ball almost round-arm and, if it is swinging, it will go very early.

For it to swing late, you need a higher action, keeping the wrist directly behind the ball and releasing it as late as possible. I was interested to hear a talk by John Trower, who coaches Steve Backley, and he said that what makes Steve such a great javelin thrower is that he releases the javelin at the last possible moment. By doing that, he finds that it not only gives him more distance but it also makes the javelin curve away slightly at the end of its flight instead of doing the normal thing and ducking inwards.

SEAM

Seam bowling is a classic English technique brought about by grassy, damp pitches which enable the seam of the ball to grip when it hits the surface and deviate one way or the other.

The latest in a long line of great English seamers is Middlesex's Angus Fraser who will just run up and bowl for over after over and try to 'hit the seam' six times out of six. Most of the time, he will not know which way the ball is going to go because that is dictated by which side of the seam hits the pitch. I have heard it said that Sir Stanley Matthews could cross a football with the lace facing away from the centre-forward who was going to head it but I haven't heard of too many seamers who could say which set of stitches the ball was going to land on.

To HIT THE SEAM, you again need a basic grip and sideways action with the wrist cocked and right behind the ball to bring it down in the same area time and time again. It obviously helps if the ball is new and hard with the seam pronounced and protruding from the surface of the ball.

Just how much difference this makes has been graphically illustrated in English cricket in recent years by the huge variations in the size of the seam. Prior to 1989, we had big, pronounced seams which coincided with a lot of grassy pitches and resulted in seam bowlers of very modest ability picking up bundles of wickets simply by running up and hitting the seam. Since 1990, the imbalance has gone the other way with a reduced seam and relatively grassless pitches making it more difficult for even the best seamers to get anybody out.

The huge gulf between these two extremes was brought home to me during a championship match between Somerset and Lancashire at Taunton in 1993. One cricket-ball manufacturer (Duke's) had introduced a ball which did not conform to the new specifications laid down by the Test and County Cricket Board but some counties still had a few on their stocks and these were used for the match. It was just like the good old days for the seamers – or the bad old days from the batsmen's point of view.

The ball seamed all over the place on a greenish pitch, Somerset's Andrew Caddick and Lancashire's Phillip DeFreitas took twelve wickets each and the match was all over an hour after tea on the second day. It was a perfect demonstration of the difference a bigger seam can make.

CUTTERS

While the seam bowler will not normally know which way the ball is going to seam after it hits the pitch, he can also bowl cutters in a deliberate attempt to make it go one way or the other. They were more prevalent in the days of uncovered pitches but they remain a potent weapon in the northern leagues and they are coming back into the first-class game.

For the OFF-CUTTER, the bowler will grip the ball as he does for the basic seamer but cut his finger down the leg side of the ball to make it go from off to leg. Bowlers like Gordon Parsons of Leicestershire and Steve Barwick of Glamorgan practise this technique and while off-cutters do not tend to be all that destructive they can be very difficult to get away.

The LEG-CUTTER, for which the bowler cuts his finger down the offside of the ball to make it go from leg to off, is more difficult to bowl, which is why it has had so few great exponents. One of them was Alec Bedser who admits that he discovered he could virtually *spin* the ball at speed quite by accident. He had been taught how to stop the new ball swinging in by holding it across the seam but, bowling to Australia's Sid Barnes in a Test match at Sydney, he was surprised to see the ball move sharply away and immediately added the leg-cutter to his armoury.

One important factor was that Alec has huge hands and fingers in which a cricket ball must have felt like a marble. To this day, if anyone asks him how to bowl a leg-cutter, his initial response is: 'Show me your hands.'

Like Alec before them, England's seam bowlers found cutters a good variation on the flat pitches of Australia in 1994–5. Once the ball has lost its newness, and particularly at a ground like Sydney, where the ball grips, cutters can be used as a good variation ball. Phillip DeFreitas, bowling off-cutters at medium pace, found this a useful ploy during the second Test at Melbourne while Darren Gough must have picked up half a dozen Test scalps with his off-cutter.

SPIN

There are two basic types of spin bowling: FINGER SPIN, which is OFF-SPIN and SLOW LEFT ARM, for which you generally use the

*Paul Adams, a
unique left arm wrist
spinner.*

index finger to make the ball rotate sideways; and WRIST SPIN, which is mainly LEG BREAKS and GOOGLIES, for which you turn over the wrist and spin the ball with the third finger.

For OFF-SPIN, you grip the ball with your first and second fingers spread apart across the seam with the thumb and third finger resting lightly underneath for support. You spin the ball as though you are turning a doorknob from left to right and after a while you should get a callus on that finger where it has rubbed against the ball.

Interestingly enough, the Australian off-spinner, Tim May, who is one of the biggest spinners in world cricket today, gets a callus on the inside of his second finger, indicating that he spins the ball off that finger. This is quite unorthodox but the most important thing is to spin the ball hard and Tim May will finish a game with a gash rather than a callus on the inside of his spinning finger, which shows how much action he puts on the ball. The more the spin, the greater the action you can put on the ball, the more it will dip and swerve in its flight and the greater the chance of deceiving the batsman.

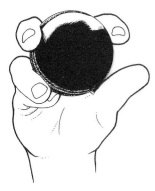

Off-spin

The off-spinner's action is sideways-on with the bowler trying to get close to the stumps so that if he gets any curve or drift through the air the ball will go from leg to off, like a gentle out-swinger, before turning back into the batsman.

This curve also produces the off-spinner's variation, the ARM BALL, which he does not try to turn but allows to go with the arm and drift towards the slips.

There is a lot of talk among off-spinners about how close they should get to the stumps. Lance Gibbs, the great West Indian bowler who was the most prolific Test wicket-taker of them all, used to bowl from very wide of the stumps; John Emburey, England's best off-spinner of recent times, sometimes gets so close that his back foot is over as far as the off stump at the bowler's end.

My view is that if the bowler gets too far across, he has to put a massive amount of spin on the ball to turn it off the straight; on the other hand, if he is too wide, he is creating an awkward angle for himself if he is to take wickets. As in most things, the answer is a happy medium with the off-spinner using the crease to vary his angle of attack and keep the batsman guessing.

Interestingly, Tim May bowled a lot round the wicket to me during the 1994–5 Ashes series. This is accepted practice when the ball is turning a great deal but he used to go round when there was no spin. When he was asked why, he shrugged and said that it was merely a different angle of attack to the one a right-handed batsman might be used to.

The SLOW LEFT ARM bowler uses the same basic grip and action as the off-spinner – unless he happens to be somebody quite unique like South Africa's Paul Adams – but, obviously, everything happens the other way round. His curve goes from off to leg, his spin from leg to off and his variation or arm ball drifts into the right-hand batsman instead of away from him.

Slow left arm

Wrist spin as practised by Adams, is a completely different technique from finger spin in that you are turning the wrist over and flipping the third finger to put even more spin on the ball. There are also more variations, which is why there has always been an air of mystery surrounding the great leg-spinners like Clarrie Grimmett, Arthur Mailey and Bill O'Reilly before the war and Bhagwat Chandrasekhar, Abdul Qadir and Shane Warne in more recent times.

The right-arm LEG-SPINNER grips the ball with the first and second fingers spread wide across the seam and the third finger bent and pressing on the side of the seam. With the wrist pointing towards cover, he spins or flips the ball with that third finger out of the back of his hand to make it turn from leg to off.

Leg-spin

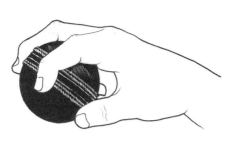

For the GOOGLY the wrist is directed more towards midwicket so that the ball turns like an off break from off to leg but the bowler will do his best to disguise this from the batsman. The object of the exercise is to bowl both the leg break and the googly with almost identical actions so that the batsman cannot pick one from the other.

Another variation is the TOP-SPINNER whereby the bowler tries to spin the ball straight on towards the batsman. For this, he will put overspin on the ball which should give it greater loop and a bigger dip and make it bounce and gather a bit more pace.

Then there is the FLIPPER which is the most difficult delivery to perfect and the most jealously guarded of all the leg-spinner's secrets. Basically, it is a back-spinner or under-spinner which is flipped out with a clicking motion between the second finger and the thumb. As the batsman sees it, it will be spinning away from him, giving it a flatter trajectory and making him think that it is a short ball when in fact it is a delivery of normal length.

Every great leg-spin bowler will have a flipper. They will guard their secret with their lives, each one being differently performed but with the same devastating effect. The intention is to get the batsman playing back when he should be forward. In Adam's case, all these variations are further complicated by the fact that he is bowling out of the back of his *left* hand so everything happens the other way round.

❝ As I'm walking back, I think maybe I'll bowl a googly. Then, as I run in, no, I'll bowl a leg-spinner. Then, do you know, just as I prepare to bowl, I decide it'll be a googly after all. And then, as I let go of the ball, I say sod it, I'll bowl a top-spinner. **❞**

BHAGWAT CHANDRASEKHAR, Indian leg-spinner

15 THE BALL

One cricket ball may look much the same as another from beyond the boundary but I can assure you that even in these days of machine manufacture and mass production their characteristics can be very different.

There are three makes of cricket ball in general use in first-class cricket these days, namely Duke's and Reader's, which are both produced by long-established English firms, and Kookaburra, which, as you may have guessed, originates from Australia and is primarily used in Australasia and, I believe, South Africa.

In England, captains tend to go with their bowlers' preference. What normally happens is that the captain and/or the senior bowler will go into the umpires' room and, in their presence, make a choice from a box of balls provided by the ground authority. At the moment, the England bowlers seem to favour Duke's balls because they think they swing more. In my experience, the Reader's seem to stay harder for longer and appear to be more conducive to reverse-swing but Phillip DeFreitas, for example, who is an out-and-out swing bowler, prefers the Duke's.

Not that we always get what we want. In England, we give touring sides a say in which make of ball is to be used and if the captains cannot agree a coin is tossed to decide. Everywhere else in the world, visiting teams do not get a choice in the matter. The home authority tells you which ball you are going to use and I cannot think why we do not do the same.

Apart from a set of new balls, the ground authority must also have a selection of older balls, marked according to how much use they have had in the past. These are required when the original ball has to be changed because it has gone out of shape or been damaged in some way. Not so long ago, we had a lot of trouble with one particular brand of balls which tended to lose their shape very early and it is not uncommon for balls to be damaged through hitting the boundary boards, a surrounding wall, the car park or even the chairman's Rolls-Royce.

It is up to the umpires to decide whether a ball has become unfit for play and should be replaced by one with a similar amount of wear but some captains will try to make them think it is just because it is not swinging and they want to try their luck with a replacement.

Changing the ball does not always work to your advantage, though, because you may finish up with a ball which is not as good as the one you had before. This happened to England when we were playing South Africa at Headingley and the ball came back from the boundary with a piece taken out of it. We had the ball changed and were given an older, softer ball which was not quite what we wanted on the kind of wicket where you needed some hardness to get any bounce or movement at all. We were not very happy about that.

There is also the question of the second new ball which is available to the fielding side after 85 overs in Test matches and 100 overs in the County Championship. You are not compelled to take it and there are times when you would rather hang on to what you have got.

The spinners may be on top. The shiny new ball is not so easy to grip and, in any case, they are bowling well, the ball is turning and you do not want to interrupt their rhythm and give the batsman any respite.

On other occasions, the old ball may be rough and scuffed on one side but still shiny and smooth on the other which will make it conducive to reverse-swing. This was the case against South Africa at Lord's in 1994 when we did not take the new ball precisely because Darren Gough preferred to bowl with the old one.

Then again, you may not want a new ball for a quite different reason. This is when you are on the receiving end. This time the batsmen are completely on top, they are dominating all the bowlers and you fear that a newer, shinier ball may disappear off the bat even faster than the old one is doing – which is what happened against New Zealand at Lord's earlier that year.

Generally speaking, however, you are ready to take the new ball once it becomes available because in most situations it will give you a better chance of taking wickets.

It is going to be harder with a more prominent seam, it is going to go through at a better pace and carry to the wicketkeeper and slips, it is going to bounce more and, with a bit of luck, you will have been able to keep your quick bowlers reasonably fresh for a renewed effort. The spinners also appreciate the extra bounce and you can take it for them as we did against Australia at Edgbaston in 1993. The ball was turning but there was not a lot of bounce so we took the new ball, gave it to the quick bowlers for a couple of overs each to get rid of some of the shine and then handed it back to the spinners.

Even spinners can do nothing with a ball which is completely soft and seamless – like the one we finished up with against Australia at

Melbourne in 1990. By the time the new ball became available, the seam on the old one had virtually disintegrated and all you could see was a series of little dots imprinted across the middle of the ball.

16 THINKING THEM OUT

All – well, almost all – the great bowlers have been thinking bowlers, intelligent cricketers who studied every batsman they played against and then used their skill and expertise to probe what they perceived to be their weaknesses.

There have been dozens of them down the years but, from my own experience, I am thinking of bowlers like Richard Hadlee, Malcolm Marshall, Terry Alderman, Allan Donald and Craig McDermott. Whenever I batted against people of their calibre, I found that they were always working you out, sometimes working you over and, more often than not, exposing your shortcomings.

I particularly remember one cross-examination by Hadlee soon after he had become Sir Richard in 1990. We were playing New Zealand in the second Test at Lord's and I had already made 151 against them at Trent Bridge, scoring a lot of runs with the forcing shot off the back foot. It was one of my more obvious strengths at the time and I would play it to balls that were short and wide of the off stump and could be hammered through the offside.

On that occasion, it had been most effective but it is also a shot which can cause you problems against the new ball because of the extra pace and bounce and Sir Richard was obviously very aware of that. He did not get much chance to explore the possibilities in the first innings at Lord's because I was bowled for nought by Danny Morrison but when I went in again on a pair he began to probe away in that area around the off stump.

How he did not get me out I will never know. I was dropped by the wicketkeeper when I flashed at one delivery, I was caught off what turned out to be a no-ball flashing again and I played and missed any number of times. All the while Sir Richard was looking to get me out in that precise area and although I eventually struggled to 50 it was only because of some enormous slices of good fortune.

Hadlee was an expert at that sort of thing, having realised, just like Lillee and Marshall did, that once the first flush of youth had left his cheeks he had to find other ways of getting batsmen out than through sheer speed.

That is how they all started, though, because pace is obviously the first weapon in any fast bowler's armoury. And, as an opening batsman, you often need a bit of luck to survive the first few deliveries when so much depends on whether you can see the ball out of the bowler's hand and pick up the line quickly enough.

If a great fast bowler – or even a very ordinary fast bowler, come to that – gets the ball in the right place at the start of an innings it can be hellishly difficult to keep it out.

Curtly Ambrose got me out first ball when we needed only 194 to beat the West Indies in Trinidad in 1994 and I have to admit that it was a delivery which would probably get me out nine times out of ten. It was a break-back at high speed on off stump and there was not a lot I could do about it.

That is the kind of thing a fast bowler must dream about because they usually have to work a bit harder for their wickets. A more typical method he will use to get a batsman out is by beating him on a length. By that, I mean he will push the batsman back by bowling short, short, short – if he can get away with it – and then deliver a ball of fuller length which will find the batsman playing back when he should be playing forward and paying the ultimate penalty.

> **Through experience, a bowler will 'feel' where a batsman is uncomfortable. It may be a certain line of attack, such as at the body, or a certain length, either full or short. The experienced bowler – and his captain – will get a feel for this and probe around those areas.**

I say 'if he can get away with it' because bowlers are supposed to be limited to only two bouncers – or 'fast, short-pitched ball' as the regulations call it – per over at the moment. For a lot of fast bowlers, the bouncer is an integral part of their attack and such legislation has done them any amount of harm. Bowlers like Devon Malcolm and Merv Hughes, for example, are just not the same bowlers with this limitation.

On the other hand, there are some fast bowlers to whom such restrictions have made very little difference because they hardly use bouncers at all. These are the SWING BOWLERS like Waqar Younis who is as quick as anybody in the world but tends to bowl a very full length and get a high proportion of his wickets either lbw or bowled.

Swing bowlers do pitch the ball up more, the top-class exponents generally swinging the ball away from the right-handed batsman, looking to draw him into playing at it and getting him caught in the slips or gully. This is why you will see batsmen trying to avoid playing at as many balls as they can early in an innings, especially if the ball is swinging away late and tempting him to play at deliveries he should be leaving alone.

A good swing bowler will also look to get a batsman out by swinging the ball the other way. He will bowl two or three outswingers in a row and then try to straighten one up and trap the batsman in front of his stumps. Terry Alderman was especially good at this – as he showed in the Ashes series of 1989 when no fewer than nineteen of his forty-one victims were lbw.

More recently, Phillip DeFreitas produced a classic example of the swing bowler's art when he was bowling to New Zealand's Martin Crowe at Trent Bridge. 'Daffy' had a very clear idea in his mind of what he wanted to do, drawing Martin wider and wider before straightening one up and getting him leg before.

Another swing bowler's ploy is to make full use of the crease, thereby varying the angle of his delivery and upsetting the batsman's rhythm. Australia's Craig McDermott is probably the fast bowler who uses the crease more cleverly than anyone else in the world today. During the 1994–5 Ashes series, when he was at the peak of his form, he would vary the angle of his attack according to how much the ball was swinging. It was a real battle to get past the new ball.

South Africa's Fanie de Villiers is also good at using the crease and, from a batsman's point of view, I certainly think an out-swing bowler who does it is a much more difficult proposition than one who just bowls straight on at the wicket from stump to stump. When he bowls from stump to stump it is easier for the batsman to leave the ball which is swinging away than when somebody like McDermott or de Villiers bowls from wide of the crease and forces you to play. But why am I telling them this?

The SEAM BOWLER will usually try to bowl in what has become known as 'the corridor of uncertainty', a term first coined by Geoff Boycott, I believe, and subsequently taken up by Micky Stewart, the former England team manager, among others.

As far as I am concerned it is the off-stump channel. Some people say it is a few inches outside of that but as a captain I don't like my seam bowlers bowling wide of the off stump for the simple reason that they are negating two ways of getting the batsman out – bowled and lbw.

I like my seam bowlers to try to hit the off stump, which is quite an attacking line, keep bowling down that channel and tie the batsmen down. Most batsmen do not like the ball on or around that off stump and if the bowler does hit the seam and the ball deviates either way there is every chance of a wicket – bowled or lbw if it nips back; caught behind or in the slips if it moves away.

The point to remember is that because the seam bowler is never sure which way the ball is going to seam, the batsman is never sure either so anything on or close to the off stump has got to be a dangerous delivery.

The classical way for the OFF-SPINNER to get the batsman out is to bowl him through 'the gate' – the gap between bat and pad as he either pushes forward defensively or tries to drive through the off-side. Off-spinners put an awful lot of thought into the line they are going to bowl with a lot depending on how much they can actually spin the ball and how much it is turning. Basically, however, they will be looking to hit off stump so the more the ball is turning, the wider of off stump they will bowl.

They will also be looking to deceive the batsmen in the air so that if he comes down the wicket and misses he will be stumped or, if he does not quite get to the pitch of the ball, he will pop it up in the air on the legside.

The SLOW LEFT ARMER, turning the ball the other way, will be hoping to get the batsman caught at slip or gully as the ball turns and takes the edge of the bat or, like the off-spinner, deceive him with his flight and fool him in the air.

And both types of finger spinner will be looking for what we call 'bat–pad' catches which come when the ball turns, or when it dips at the end of its flight, takes the inside edge of the bat and flicks off the pad to one of the close fielders just in front of the wicket. These can be the most difficult catches for the umpire to detect because sometimes there is only the slightest deflection off the bat on to the pad, sometimes the ball takes the pad before it touches the bat – and sometimes it doesn't touch the bat at all. In that case it is not out – but not always!

When it comes to thinking batsmen out, no bowler puts more thought into it than the LEG-SPINNER who has more tricks than anybody and must try to choose the right moment to use one of his variations.

His stock delivery which turns from leg to off is dangerous enough. The classic example of that was Shane Warne's very first ball of the

1989 Ashes series which turned from outside Mike Gatting's leg stump to hit the top of off and send a shockwave through English cricket.

The orthodox leg break can also have the batsman caught behind by the wicketkeeper or in the slips or beat him in the air for a stumping. And then there are the variations which make it so difficult for the batsman to defend against the leg-spinner.

The batsman can choose not to play the leg break, knowing that if it pitches outside the leg stump he cannot be lbw and if it is straight it is likely to turn and miss the stumps altogether. But then he is vulnerable to the googly which is not so safe to leave alone because if it lands in the right area it will turn back and hit the stumps.

If a batsman tries to play low in an attempt to smother the spin, he can be confounded by the top-spinner which bounces more and will probably take the glove or the shoulder of the bat and pop up to one of the close fielders. And if a batsman decides on a policy of playing back, the top leg-spinner will produce the flipper which will shoot through low and either creep under his bat or trap him in front of the stumps.

All these considerations go through a leg-spinner's mind and it is knowing which delivery to bowl and when to bowl it that makes Shane Warne one of the most dangerous bowlers in modern cricket.

Finally we come to the OCCASIONAL BOWLER which would be a bit like going from the sublime to the ridiculous if it was not for the fact that he can be very useful on occasions. He is usually introduced to the attack when you have run out of ideas for getting a batsman out and bring him on almost as an after-thought. He might be a medium pacer or some kind of spinner who does not bowl very often and does not often get anybody out when he does but he is always worth a go if a big partnership has developed and you want to try to break the batsmen's concentration.

And it is a move which does pay off sometimes. I have got out to some very occasional bowlers in my time – people like Paul Parker of Sussex and Durham and Warwickshire's Andy Moles, to name but two.

More famous partnership-breakers were Geoff Boycott, who used to bowl with his cap back to front in an attempt to make the batsmen think he was a joke bowler when he could actually purvey some pretty nifty in-swing, and Alan Smith, now the chief executive of the Test and County Cricket Board, who was not really an occasional bowler at all. He was primarily a wicketkeeper-batsman for Warwickshire and England but he took 131 wickets in his career with his brisk, windmilling medium pace, including a hat-trick when he took his pads off and had a bowl against Essex. Keith

Geoff Boycott – his bowling was no joke.

Fletcher, the England team manager, was his third victim!

More recently, I brought Mark Ramprakash on to bowl his occasional off-spin when Brian Lara was going well against England in Guyana. The West Indian genius, obviously thinking that 'Ramps' could not bowl at all, danced down the pitch and was astonished when the ball turned past his bat. Unfortunately Jack Russell was just as surprised and missed the stumping!

> **❝** I used to give every new batsman four balls. One was a bouncer to check his courage, the second a fizzer to check his eyesight, the third was a slow 'un to try out his reflexes and the fourth a bender to see if he was a good cricketer. And if he took a single off each of the four balls I knew I was in trouble. **❞**
>
> England fast bowler HAROLD LARWOOD

17 CHOOSING AN END

Before a captain leads his team on to the field, he should have discussed with his bowlers which end they want to bowl from. This may seem a relatively trivial matter but it is not because he wants to wave to his wife or girlfriend or have his best side facing the camera. It is much more important than that.

There are various reasons why a bowler will want to operate from a particular end – or why, on the odd occasion, his captain will overrule him. Ideally you will want him to bowl at the end where he feels happiest but there are other factors to be taken into consideration, among them the slope, the wind and perhaps even the umpire, as well as superstition and the habit of a lifetime.

The most famous SLOPE in the cricket world is at Lord's where the ground falls by more than eight feet from the grandstand side down to where the old Tavern used to be and by about three feet across the square itself. It even causes problems for batsmen, never mind bowlers. Batting at the Nursery End, where the slope is from off to leg, the right-hand batsman is drawn into playing at balls he should not be playing at because he is constantly aware of the ball moving into him, i.e. down the slope, and he cannot leave it with any confidence. Alternatively, batting at the Pavilion End with the slope from leg to off he is tempted into playing wide off the stump at balls which are leaving him as they move down the slope.

The bowlers, meanwhile, have to decide how the slope will suit them best. It is a relatively easy matter for the spinners. The off-spinner will want to bowl from the Pavilion End so that he is turning the ball down the slope and the leg-spinner or slow left armer will prefer the Nursery End because he is obviously turning the ball the other way. But for the quicker bowlers it is not so simple.

You would think they would prefer to bowl from the Nursery End where the slope will help them to move the ball away from the batsman. Yet most seam bowlers like Angus Fraser and swing bowlers like Phillip DeFreitas who have done a lot of bowling at Lord's in both Test and county cricket will tell you that the Pavilion End is the only place to bowl from.

One fairly obvious reason is that the infamous 'ridge' which was supposed to be responsible for some notorious Lord's pitches a few years ago was at the Nursery End. They say that it was caused by the drainage system and has since been ironed out by the re-laying of the square but, cricket being the game it is, the ridge is still a factor in players' thinking.

A more valid explanation why out-swing bowlers can be more effective bowling against the slope was provided by New Zealand's Dion Nash when he took eleven wickets in the Lord's Test of 1994. He could still get the odd ball to move away *up* the slope and because the batsmen were aware that it was always likely to nip back *down* the slope and trap them lbw they were much more likely to play at the out-swinger.

If bowlers like Nash or DeFreitas bowled from the Nursery End, the batsmen might play and miss a lot more as the swing and the slope took the ball away from them, but they would not get as many nicks as they would at the other end.

A Test ground with more of a HILL than a slope is Headingley where bowlers have to run in downhill from the Kirkstall Lane End and uphill from the Football Stand End and find that the gradient can cause them major problems. Those who come hurtling down the hill find that they are constantly over-stepping the crease and being no-balled; those who struggle up the hill find that they are not quite reaching the mark and have difficulty settling into any kind of rhythm.

All the bowlers can do is try to come to terms with the problems in their own way but for those who suffer from no-ball trouble at the best of times Headingley can be a real nightmare. England's Derek Pringle, for example, used to try all sorts of things in his efforts to stop himself from over-stepping. After one game in which he had bowled well and not given away too many no-balls, he took some string out to the middle and cut it to the exact length of the run he had used. He would take that piece of string around with him and use it to measure his run but it still did not cure his problem. As he said, there are so many variables when a bowler is trying to find his rhythm, including the undulations of the ground, and especially at Headingley.

The most famous WIND in the cricket world is the Fremantle Doctor, the stiff sea breeze which pays a daily call to the WACA in Perth as if by appointment and blows throughout the hours of play. Touring teams know what to expect and since it blows directly across the ground it is a simple decision to give the advantage to the out-swing bowler.

At my home ground, Old Trafford, it is a different matter. There the wind almost always blows straight down the pitch and the bowler given the choice of ends will opt to bowl with the breeze at his back because it is so much easier and will leave his second string to labour into the breeze at the other end. Yet the ball will often swing more against the wind because there is greater resistance and pull and, ironically, the bowler who has to do the donkey work will get the greater reward.

There are times when bowlers will want a particular end for reasons other than the slope and the wind. Some of them like to bowl from the end where a certain umpire is standing. He will not mind me mentioning it because he often takes the mickey out of himself but Ray Julien, the former Leicestershire wicketkeeper who is now one of England's most experienced umpires, is one who, shall we say, is not afraid of giving batsmen out, so bowlers like to bowl at his end.

Then there are bowlers who favour a particular end through habit or superstition and this is when captains sometimes have to draw the line. Devon Malcolm has always told me that when he is playing at the Oval he likes to bowl from the Vauxhall End because it is lucky for him. Unfortunately – or fortunately, as things turned out – I had to give DeFreitas that end when we played South Africa there in 1994 and Devon had to bowl from the Pavilion End, whether he liked it or not. He finished up with 9 for 57, thereby proving that habit and superstition are not the most important criteria when it comes to success on the cricket field.

18 SETTING THE FIELD

There is a lovely story about Keith Miller, the great Australian all-rounder whose happy-go-lucky approach to the game probably derived from the fact that cricket cannot have seemed all that important when you had been a fighter pilot during the war. Apparently Keith was captaining New South Wales when it was pointed out to him that he had led twelve players on to the field. 'OK,' he said decisively, 'one of you bugger off and the rest scatter.'

For most of us, the business of getting the fielders in the right positions is a bit more complex than that. It depends on a variety of things such as the type of bowler who is bowling, the ability of the batsman, the condition and pace of the pitch and the state of the game. But there are conventional fields which a captain would set for different kinds of bowlers and I will try to explain these as simply as I can.

BASIC FIELDS

At the start of an innings, a FAST BOWLER armed with the new ball on a reasonably quick wicket would basically want a fair number of close catchers, so you would start with three slips, a gully and a short leg. You would have a fine leg, a mid-on – or, if the pitch was particularly quick, a man behind square on the legside. A cover and a mid-off would complete the field.

This is what we call a 6–3 field – that is six fielders on the offside and three on the legside – and it might vary according to the state of the pitch and the style of the batsman. You could have two slips and two gullies for someone who likes to cut; you could move the man at mid-on or behind square into a closer catching position, perhaps leg slip or short fine leg, if the pitch was really quick. Generally speaking, however, fast bowlers prefer to have a mid-on because it gives them a bit more leeway if they want to pitch the ball up and they do not like the batsman driving them through there.

Right arm fast

1. Wicketkeeper
2. 1st Slip
3. 2nd Slip
4. 3rd Slip
5. Gully
6. Short Leg
7. Cover
8. Mid-Off
9. Fine Leg
10. Bowler
*11. Mid-On/ Backward Square

* Depending on pitch and p of bowler

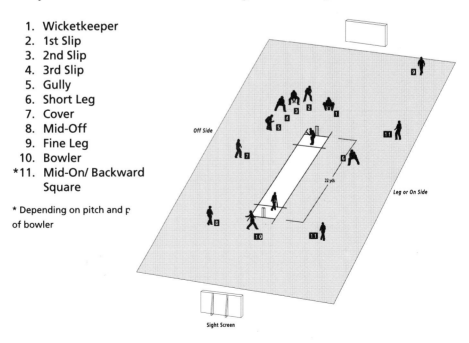

One of the criticisms of my captaincy during the 1994–5 Ashes tour was that often I did not have enough close catchers around the bat. While I would reckon the criticism to be harsh at times, especially when we were up against it at Brisbane, I believe I could have been more attacking in the second innings at Melbourne. We were 60 runs adrift and I gave Devon Malcolm two slips, a gully and a short leg. Perhaps I ought to have been more attacking. Our only chance of victory was to take wickets and, psychologically, our bowlers might have been more aggressive

An OUT-SWING bowler would have a similar sort of field to a fast bowler. He may want a third man if the ball is swinging significantly and have to bowl to a 7–2 field but, generally, I don't like doing that because it can make the bowler bowl too wide. We had this problem with Phillip DeFreitas against South Africa at Lord's in 1994. He was bowling beautifully from the Nursery End, the out-swing taking the ball down the slope, but with a 7–2 field he was bowling slightly *too* wide and the batsman just kept playing and missing or leaving the ball. If we had had a slightly more conventional field with a bit more cover on the legside he may have been inclined to start the ball straighter and get the nicks to the slips which we were looking for. Alternatively, he could have bowled from the Pavilion End, where, as I explained earlier, the batsman would have been wary of the ball coming back down the slope and would have played at it more often.

For an IN-SWING bowler you would be looking to strengthen the

In-swing

1. Wicketkeeper
2. 1st Slip
3. 2nd Slip
4. Gully
5. Cover
6. Mid-Off
7. Bowler
8. Fine Leg
9. Short Leg / Short Midwicket
10. Backward Square
11. Mid-On

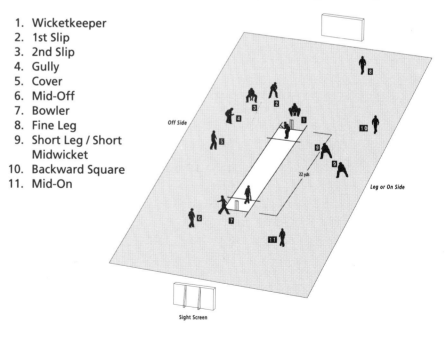

legside. In this case, you might have a 5–4 field with two slips and a gully, a leg gully for the clip round the corner off the batsman's legs, a short leg, a square leg and a mid-on with just a cover point and a mid-off for protection on the offside.

The field for the OFF-SPINNER is slightly more complicated. In England, off-spin bowlers tend to adopt a somewhat negative line, bowling at middle-and-off with a 6–3 *legside* field, that is with six men on the legside and just three on the offside. The close catchers would be a slip for the arm ball, a silly point for those bat–pad catches on the offside and, if the ball was turning a little, a short leg. If the ball was turning more, or if the batsman was playing with his bat well out in front of his pad, you would consider having a leg slip.

Off-spin – Test Match

1. Wicketkeeper
2. Slip
3. Point
4. Extra Cover
5. Mid-Off
6. Bowler
7. Silly Point
8. Deep Backward Square
9. Midwicket
10. Mid-On
11. Short Leg

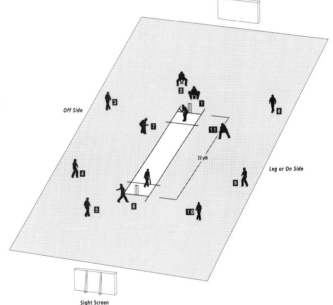

When the ball is turning and the batsman decides that the best form of defence is attack, off-spinners will often have what we call an 'in-out' field. You still have those two or three catchers around the bat but you also have a couple of 'scouts' out on the boundary edge to stop the batsman going for fours. In this way, you hope to catch him in between or half-and-half.

The Australian off-spinners, in particular, do things differently. They bowl a much more attacking line and, accordingly, have a different field. Whereas the English off-spinner bowls at middle-and-off to a legside field, an Australian like Tim May will often bowl to a 5–4 or even a 6–3 *offside* field, pitching the ball well outside the off stump and trying to hit that stump. It is very unlike the English approach and requires a different kind of technique and outlook from the batsman. A legitimate shot against this type of attack, for example, is the old-fashioned slog with the spin over the legside fielders.

A bowler turning the ball away from the bat, a LEG-SPINNER or a LEFT ARM SPINNER, would bowl with a 6–3 offside field, his close catchers being a slip, a gully and a bat–pad with a mid-off and a man on the drive at short extra cover. On the legside, he would have a man on the sweep, a midwicket and a mid-on.

Slow left arm

1. Wicketkeeper
2. Slip
3. Bowler
4. Deep Backward Square
5. Midwicket
6. Mid-On
7. Mid-Off
8. Extra Cover
9. Point
10. Cover
11. Silly Point/Short Extra Cover

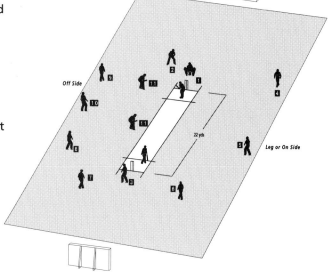

Shane Warne, however, prefers to bowl a much straighter line and strengthens his legside field accordingly. This gives him two advantages: greater room for error with the short ball so it cannot be cut through the offside; and, because he turns the ball so much and has a dangerous flipper, he is attacking the stumps more frequently. During the last Ashes tour, Phil Tufnell also bowled often with a predominantly legside field, landing the ball into the rough created by the bowlers. Apart from the fact that he would get greater purchase out of that rough, some of the free-scoring Australian batsmen did not like the ploy because it reduced their scoring options and increased the number of risks they might have to take. I suppose this is being negative in order to take wickets.

Leg spin – Shane Warne

1. Wicketkeeper
2. Slip
3. Silly Point
4. Bowler
5. Deep Backward Square
* 6. Short Fine Leg / Cover
7. Midwicket
8. Mid-On
9. Mid-Off
10. Extra Cover
11. Point

* Depending on the line of attack the bowler uses

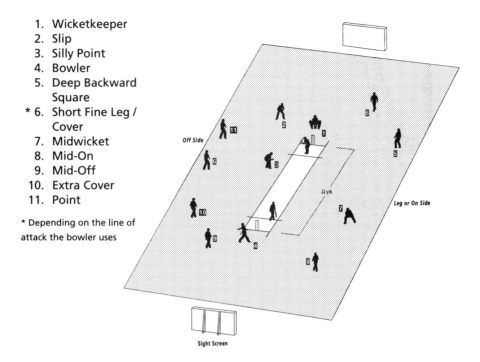

POSITIONAL SENSE

One of the main things a captain has to take into account when setting the field is the pace of the pitch. On a SLOW pitch, you generally want your fielders who are backward of square, or behind the wicket, to move squarer or, in some cases, in front of square. Your wicketkeeper and slips would also move closer to the stumps because the ball would not carry as far, although the gully catcher would actually drop deeper because he would be less likely to get a catch off the gloves or the splice of the bat than from a full-blooded slash.

On a QUICK pitch, you ask the fielders to go finer, the wicketkeeper and slips go deeper and the gully catcher moves in for that catch off the gloves or splice. Third man can also become a crucial position. Instead of being just a run-saver, he can be a catcher as well if he comes in ten or fifteen yards. I remember asking Steve Watkin to do this against Australia at the Oval in 1993 and it almost paid off when Shane Warne carved a ball over the slips and it only just evaded him.

On pitches without any pace at all, you might despair of ever getting anyone out in the traditional ways like caught behind or in the slips and move your fielders into all sorts of unconventional positions. This happened at Melbourne in 1991 when both captains, Allan Border and Graham Gooch, felt that the ball would never go to the close catchers. They finished up with only one slip or no slip at all and just fiddled around with their fielders in silly positions, such as in the batsman's line of sight, in their desperate attempts to get a wicket.

PUTTING ON THE PRESSURE

All the fielding variations depend, of course, on how the game is going. If you are on top, you are looking to attack with plenty of catchers around the bat to keep the pressure on the opposition. If, on the other hand, the batting side is on top and you are under pressure yourself, you have to sit back and defend and try to get a wicket that way. Some batsmen are very free scoring and hate to be bogged down. If they are, they can give you their wicket through a rash shot. In ONE-DAY MATCHES, especially, the fielding side is often under tremendous pressure and will try to reverse that pressure by bowling to a pre-set plan.

Much depends on the state of the pitch and whether the ball is swinging or seaming early in the innings but, generally speaking, you do not attack so much in one-day cricket. You might start with a couple of slips but it is not too long before the 'sweepers'– a relatively new term which has come in to the game with the development of one-day cricket – are posted on the boundary edge. You might have one on the offside, just in front of cover point, and another on the legside, normally just backward of square.

It is purely defensive positions like these which make limited-overs cricket such a stereotyped game and not a patch on the real thing – although there are times when you are forced to resort to similar measures in Test matches. The wicket may be flat, the ball old, the batsmen well set and, rather than wait for the odd magic delivery or 'jaffa' to come along and get you a wicket, you have to try to exert pressure on the batsman by making him work for every run. We did this against the West Indies in Trinidad in 1994 when the greenness had gone from the pitch, the hardness had gone from the ball and Keith Arthurton and Jimmy Adams had put on a few in their second innings.

We badly needed a wicket and I asked Andrew Caddick to bowl me five or six overs at Keith Arthurton costing no more than two runs an over. I knew that Arthurton was the kind of batsman who likes to keep the scoreboard ticking over and might make a mistake if we could tie him down. So I wanted Andy to bowl fairly straight with just one slip and a ring of fielders and see if we could just cut off his flow of runs. Sure enough, in Andy's fifth over, Arthurton got a ball that was slightly short but not short enough to pull and when he went for the shot he lobbed up a catch to midwicket.

It was a classic case of a bowler following a captain's advice and getting a wicket – not with a great delivery but through sheer pressure on the batsman.

Dominic Cork, whose emergence should strengthen England all round.

STRENGTHS AND WEAKNESSES

I like to know about the batsmen we are playing against, where they score their runs, where they tend to hit the ball in the air, that kind of thing, and, as a team, we have long discussions about them. We have meetings the night before a game and during the lunch and tea intervals, talking to the bowlers about where to bowl at certain batsmen in order to get them out, where not to bowl because that is where they are particularly strong and where to have the fielders, either in catching or run-saving positions.

Sometimes you are forced to go into a series 'blind' and I hate it. When we played New Zealand in 1994, I didn't know too many of their players so I made a special trip to watch them playing in a game at Lord's to try to get an idea of how they played. Against

South Africa, it was even worse. I did not know much about them at all at the start of the series and I wasn't very happy about it.

One player we did know about was New Zealand's Mark Greatbatch and when he returned to their side for the third Test at Old Trafford we were ready for him. His weakness at that time against the short ball was common knowledge in the cricket world and on a quick, bouncy pitch we just 'bombed' him into submission in both innings.

Normally, you have to do a bit more homework than that. In the West Indies earlier that year we thought long and hard about how we were going to bowl to their left-handers, Brian Lara, Jimmy Adams and Keith Arthurton, and while the results may not have looked all that spectacular we did talk about them very carefully. We came to the conclusion that they are not like most left-handers who are habitually strong on the legside. What they liked was plenty of width outside the off stump. They liked to get forward and flay the ball through the offside so we tried to bowl much straighter at them.

They had their individual traits as well. As I said earlier, Arthurton is one of those dashing, quick-scoring batsmen like Australia's Mark Waugh and South Africa's Jonty Rhodes who hate to be bottled up and can be pressurised into doing something rash. Jimmy Adams is hardly in that category. He likes to play forward so you encourage the bowlers to let him have the odd bouncer; he often plays a stiff-legged drive so you might have a man at short extra cover for the catch; and he tends to lunge forward so you may have a silly mid-off to deter him. As for Brian Lara, you stress to your bowlers and sometimes even plead with them not to give him too much width on the offside. You want them to bowl straight, even as straight as middle-and-leg, because he likes to flick the ball down the legside and can be caught there.

On that Caribbean tour, our team manager, Keith Fletcher, would give me detailed charts from the scorer, Alex Davis, showing where batsmen were scoring their runs. If Richie Richardson had got 50, Keith would show me his chart afterwards, saying: 'Look at this … see how seventy per cent of his runs came behind square on the offside.' Another chart that springs to mind showed how Desmond Haynes had scored seventy-five per cent of his runs behind square on the legside, so it was crucial to have a run-saver in that position.

I also make my own notes on players I have seen in county cricket or come across in Test matches and keep a little file on them at home. Just picking one out at random, I find a few details about Shivnarine Chanderpaul, the young Guyanese left-hander who made his Test debut against us in the West Indies. According to my notes, he is strong square of the wicket, he likes the short ball, he likes to pull and cut. He has got a loose driving technique and often nicks it when driving or pushing forward. The ball should therefore be bowled from over the wicket at a fullish length towards his off stump to try to get him driving. He likes to clip the ball behind square on the legside so that has got to be a run-saving position. He also chips it in the air so on a quick wicket you might fancy a leg gully. Against the left arm spinner, he often hits the ball in the air to the man on the drive on the legside. Details like these will refresh my memory and, I hope, stand us in good stead the next time we play against him.

PRE-PLANNING It is very gratifying, of course, when you get a batsman out as a direct result of something you have planned with your bowlers and fielders beforehand, where you have taken advice from a respected colleague or simply where you have followed your own instinct. The following are four specific examples during my time as England captain – plus one where the plan did not quite work out.

Observation A classic example of a pre-planned wicket was the dismissal of Stuart Williams when he made his debut for the West Indies in the final Test in Antigua in 1994. We had played against him in the Leeward Islands game and noticed very early in his innings that he was always ready to have a go at hooking bouncers that were fairly straight and fairly high. Angus Fraser had hardly bowled a bouncer throughout the tour but he gave him one straight away and Williams obligingly hooked the ball straight to Andy Caddick, the only fielder we had out for the hook, at deep backward square leg. Mind you, I don't know why we bothered. Brian Lara came in next …

Trap Some batsmen already have a reputation for being fond of the hook shot, among them the West Indies captain, Richie Richardson. It is very much a West Indian trait to take on the bouncers so when he hooked out in the first Test at Sabina Park to a man deliberately placed for him it was a great psychological success for us. We felt that he had fallen into our trap and from then on we put a man out for the hook in the belief that he would not be able to resist it. Often he did not resist and was caught there again or just managed to clear the fielder. It was always in the back of our minds that he liked to hook – and it was always in the back of his mind that the fielder was there.

Advice A captain should always be ready to take advice from his vice-captain, his wicketkeeper – England's Jack Russell, for instance, is an excellent source of information about what the ball is doing and how the bowlers are bowling – and his senior players. I did this against Australia at the Oval in 1993 when we had only about twenty overs left to bowl them out and Merv Hughes was hanging around and beginning to get on our nerves. Graham Gooch came up to me and suggested that Angus Fraser should go round the wicket with a short leg and two men back for the hook and bowl a kind of leg theory at him. At once Merv was uncomfortable and shortly afterwards hooked the ball down Steve Watkin's throat at fine leg.

Instinct

Sometimes a captain will do something purely by instinct and it pays off – as it did for me against South Africa at Lord's in 1994. I had gone into the game not knowing about their opening batsman, Andrew Hudson, or how he played, but Darren Gough gave him a bit of a roughing up at the start and it was soon clear that he did not play the short stuff too well. I immediately put a man at short leg and another round the corner on the legside and instructed Goughy to keep banging the ball in. Glancing round the field, I realised that Angus Fraser was at fine leg. Since Hudson looked as though he was just about at the end of his tether in trying to fend the ball off and likely to have a go with the hook at any moment, I decided to swap Angus with Graham Gooch because he was likely to be a bit more mobile and have better hands. Next ball, Hudson went for the hook, top-edged it and Goochy did not let me down, by running round and taking an excellent catch.

Oops ...

During team meetings we often talk about the opposition and their strengths and weaknesses. Naturally it is better to emphasise their weak points but against South Africa in 1994 I felt it was appropriate that I should mention the strength of their middle-order so we guarded against complacency as soon as we had them five wickets down. Unfortunately our bowlers became almost paranoid bowling at the likes of Brian McMillan and Craig Matthews. During the Headingley Test, Matthews cuffed our seamers around merrily, virtually saving the game for his side, and I felt that maybe the pre-planning on that occasion had raised a few negative thoughts in our bowlers' minds. Unfortunately some of them still seemed to be there when we got to South Africa in 1995.

---

66 I only have to perch myself at short leg and just stare at some of 'em to get 'em out. They fiddle about and look away and then they look back to see if I'm still staring at 'em. I am. They don't stay long. **99**

BRIAN CLOSE, former Yorkshire and England captain

---

19 HAS SPIN A FUTURE?

*Jim Laker – ten
wickets in an innings.*

The only bowler to have taken all ten wickets in a Test match innings was Jim Laker, an off-spinner. The best analysis ever returned in first-class cricket (10 for 10) was by Hedley Verity, a left arm spinner. The top wicket-takers in the history of the game were Wilfred Rhodes (4,187), a left arm spinner, and 'Tich' Freeman (3,776), a leg-spinner.

But where are they now, the great – and the not-so-great – spin bowlers? And, if you can find them, have they a future?

They are questions that have frequently been asked in recent years and especially in England where, for a time, much of the legislation seemed specifically designed to make them extinct.

Look at the experience of Peter Such, one of the best off-spinners we have had in recent years. He made his first-class debut for Nottinghamshire in 1982, moved on to Leicestershire in 1987 and was not really appreciated until he arrived at Essex in 1990, finally winning his county cap the following year and an England cap two years after that.

It was Peter's misfortune that he was trying to build a career as a spin bowler in a period when English cricket was being dominated by seam bowling. Apart from the fact that Notts had Eddie Hemmings, during his time at Trent Bridge, bowlers like Clive Rice and Sir Richard Hadlee generally reigned supreme on pitches which might have been tailored to their specifications. When he went to Grace Road, Jonathan Agnew, Phillip DeFreitas and Les Taylor were revelling in conditions loaded in favour of the seamers.

Those were the days of damp, grassy pitches and balls with huge, protruding seams which led to a profusion of quick and not-so-quick bowlers who were picking up bundles of wickets and threatening to make the spinners extinct.

Other factors were conspiring against them as well. Bats were becoming heavier and heavier, with people like Graham Gooch carrying clubs which weighed three pounds and more, and on some of the smaller grounds were weapons of mass destruction as far as the spinners were concerned.

Once upon a time, any self-respecting spinner could almost guarantee that he would mop up the tail-enders – nine, ten and jack,

" If I came into the game now, I'd probably end up as a medium-pace dobber. "

FRED TITMUS, former Middlesex and England off-spinner and now a selector, 1982

as they called them – but now even the rabbits at the bottom of the batting-order no longer waltz down the pitch and throw their wickets away. Most of them these days are quite adept at thrusting a pad down the wicket, safe in the knowledge that they cannot be out lbw if the ball pitches outside the leg stump or if they are playing a shot to a ball pitching outside the off stump.

But wait. There are signs that things are changing and the spinners are on their way back. The introduction of four-day cricket in the County Championship on pitches which are generally better than those we had in the late eighties means that counties now go into matches with at least one spinner and sometimes two.

It has not gone unnoticed that the most successful counties of the nineties – Essex and Middlesex, who each won the championship twice – had two good spinners winning matches for them. When Essex won the title in 1992, John Childs and the aforementioned Peter Such took 103 wickets between them; when Middlesex won it in 1993, John Emburey and Phil Tufnell picked up a total of 127. Even when Warwickshire took the championship in 1994 on the strength of Brian Lara's batting and Tim Munton's seam bowling, they still owed a lot to their two spinners – Neil Smith and Richard Davis – who shared 80 wickets.

In Test cricket, too, the spinners are coming back into their own after years of domination by the fast bowlers. When we were trounced 3–0 in India in 1992–3, it was the spin bowling trio of Kumble, Raju and Chauhan which brought about our downfall; when Australia beat England in 1993, the architects of their victory were the spinners, Shane Warne and Tim May; and South Africa added a new dimension to their attack in 1995–6 when they brought in Paul Adams.

Now England are looking to a new breed of spin bowlers, led by Such and Tufnell but also including the likes of Richard Illingworth, Shaun Udal, Min Patel, Ian Salisbury and Richard Stemp, to bring their skills to bear on the Test match scene.

And, yes, I do think they have a future.

STYLES OF THE GAME

20 TEST CRICKET –
THE ULTIMATE CHALLENGE

It is one of cricket's great anomalies that the World Cup, the supreme championship in any other sport, is decided by a series of one-day internationals, when any top player will tell you that the ultimate examination of his ability comes in a five-day Test match. Many of the spectators who flock in their thousands to the limited-overs contests may not believe this but it is undeniably true. So why should this be?

I suppose that what makes cricket such a great game – indeed, to those who play and watch, the *greatest* game – is summed up by one of its oldest clichés, 'the glorious uncertainty'.

While one-day cricket matches consistently produce the closest, most dramatic finishes, they are rarely unpredictable. Almost every game follows a similar formula and takes on a familiar pattern. Nothing illustrated this better than the two Texaco Trophy matches between England and South Africa in 1994. Even though they were quite tense – especially the second one at Old Trafford when Graham Thorpe and Steve Rhodes pulled things round after we had lost early wickets – they were so predictable that they might have been scripted in advance.

Test cricket is not like that. It can be gloriously unpredictable, gloriously uncertain. What other sport could produce a turnaround like the Headingley Test of 1981 when England, following on against Australia, beat odds of 500–1 against to win the match? Who would have bet against Australia at Sydney in 1994 when they needed only 66 to beat South Africa with nine wickets in hand and lost by five runs? And who would have thought that England, having outplayed the West Indies for three days in Trinidad, would lose the match in inside 20 overs when they were bowled out for 46 with Curtly Ambrose producing one of the greatest fast bowling performances of all time?

Unlike one-day cricket, Test cricket is a game where *all* the skills come in to play.

- The fast bowlers are not prohibited from bowling bouncers or shackled by the need for accuracy and control, the very reasons why England often leave Devon Malcolm out of their one-day side.
- The spinners are encouraged to take wickets because you only win Test matches by bowling the other side out twice whereas one-day cricket is all about containment and stopping the flow of runs.
- Batsmen tend to hit more boundaries because the fields are not so deeply set and there are more gaps to be found.
- There are more fielders around the bat so you see more thrilling catches in the slips and gully.

All the most memorable matches I have played in have been Test

Angus Fraser – memories are made of his eight wickets in Barbados.

> **❝ Test cricket is not a light-hearted business – especially that between England and Australia. ❞**
>
> SIR DONALD BRADMAN

matches. There were those three famous victories at the Oval – against the West Indies in 1991 when Phil Tufnell took 6 wickets for 4 runs in 33 balls; against Australia in 1993 when Angus Fraser came back after injury to bowl us to victory in only my second Test as captain; and against South Africa in 1994 when Devon Malcolm took 9 for 57. Then there was that historic victory in Barbados earlier in 1994 when Alec Stewart made two centuries in the match and Angus Fraser took eight wickets.

All the top players definitely prefer Test cricket to the one-day variety. They regard Test match performances as the true yardstick of their calibre and it was significant that when David Gower decided to have a break in 1987 he opted to miss the World Cup rather than an important Test series. It is a pity that we cannot have a World Cup of Test cricket, based on teams' performances against each other over a certain period of time.

Apart from anything else, one-day internationals have become ten-a-penny these days. Some relatively young players in Australia have already played in more than a hundred internationals and I noticed when we played South Africa in 1994 that although they had been back in world cricket for only two years some of their top players had already made around fifty appearances.

I had been playing for England for five years and played in fewer than twenty. One reason was that I had not been a regular in the one-day side because I was regarded as being more of a Test match player – which I took as a compliment – but it also had something to do with the Test and County Cricket Board's stand in restricting the number of limited-overs games we play. We have to go along with what our hosts want to some extent when we are on tour but we limit the amount we play at home in an effort to preserve the status of Test cricket and I think it is a very laudable policy.

No country plays more one-day cricket than Australia – Allan Border had played in an incredible 273 games when he retired – and no country promotes the game more vigorously. Yet I am told that when Australia were narrowly beaten by Pakistan in the Karachi Test not so long ago, the players sat in the dressing room in stunned silence for more than an hour.

That shows how much Test matches mean to cricketers. You are aware of the growing tension from the beginning of the build-up a couple of days beforehand to the start of the game. The match itself is mentally and physically exhausting. But when it is all over, it seems so much more satisfying and worthwhile than any other form of cricket.

21 COUNTY CRICKET –
CHANGE FOR THE BETTER

The County Championship is the oldest and most important competition in English cricket. It may not draw the crowds like its younger, more attractive one-day offspring but for more than a hundred years it was the backbone of our game. It is precisely because it has been seen as more of a soft underbelly in recent times that it has had to undergo a major overhaul.

I have only been playing at county level since 1987 but even in that short period there have been a number of major changes:

- In 1987, we played twenty-four three-day matches on pitches which were left uncovered during the hours of play, although the bowlers' run-ups were protected from the elements.
- From 1988 until 1992, we played a mixture of sixteen three-day and six four-day games on covered pitches.
- And since 1993 we have had a programme of seventeen four-day games with the counties playing each other once.

All this is a far cry from the traditional county game. Already, the older generation looks back nostalgically to 'the good old days' when three-day cricket on uncovered pitches produced strong county teams and great England cricketers.

DECLINE

Some people trace the decline of the championship back to the proliferation of one-day cricket since the introduction of the first one-day competition, the Gillette Cup, in 1963, others to the switch to full covering of pitches in 1981.

Whatever the reasons, the championship was not serving its purpose of producing cricket and cricketers of the highest possible standard and this has been reflected by England's lack of success at Test match level over the past decade. Despite the presence of outstanding players like Ian Botham, David Gower and Graham Gooch, England were mostly unsuccessful, capable of beating the minnows of Test cricket but hard pressed even to hold their own against sides like the West Indies and Australia.

It was only in the mid-eighties, the early years of Allan Border's captaincy when Australia were trying to regroup following the loss of so many players to Kerry Packer's World Series Cricket and 'rebel' tours of South Africa, that England had any real hold on the Ashes, which have always been regarded as the acid test of our cricketing standards.

Such a lack of success led people to believe that the very basis of our first-class game, the County Championship, left a lot to be desired – and they were right.

It is a fact that our decline as a major cricketing power goes a lot deeper than that, right down to the grass roots level where all sorts of factors like the erosion of cricket in schools, the loss of playing fields, and the lure of other sports have mitigated against the national summer game. But that is another subject altogether.

THE PROBLEMS

As far as county cricket is concerned, and that is what we are discussing here, there are very real problems.

There are too many players, for a start. Bobby Simpson, the Australian coach, said in a *Daily Express* column that there were never more than thirty players in any one Test-playing country who could be considered good enough to play Test match cricket. Now I am not sure how many players there are on county staffs at the present time but it is probably ten times as many as that. It stands to reason that only a very small percentage of them are ever going to play for England so they lack the ambition and the motivation to go on and realise their full potential.

The talent, then, is spread too thinly. At each of the eighteen counties, there may be four or five top-quality players with the rest never going to be good enough to play Test cricket. They are happy enough with their lot, content to make their thousand runs or take their fifty wickets in a season and enjoy what is a very pleasant career. But many have no aspirations beyond that.

In countries like Australia and the West Indies where they have only half a dozen first-class sides, the talent is much more concentrated and the level of competition that much fiercer.

I still believe that we have more talent in England than anywhere else in the world but our cricket lacks that bite and intensity. You often see quality batsmen getting out to poor shots, top-class bowlers delivering ordinary spells, and it is simply because the standard of cricket is not testing enough.

We also play too much. County cricketers play six or seven days a week for almost six months and it is impossible to sustain the intensity of your cricket over that length of time. Players lose their edge, their sharpness, and standards drop even further.

It is partly because of this lack of competitiveness and partly because of the treadmill they find themselves on that so many English cricketers find it a lot harder to make the jump into Test cricket than their counterparts overseas. Just look at Michael Slater, the young Australian opening batsman, who played in his first Ashes series in England in 1993. In his very first Test innings at Old Trafford, he looked as though he was on his natural stage – and he proved it in his second Test at Lord's by making 150. Then look at the way Mark Lathwell and John Crawley, for example, struggled in their first few Test matches.

I believe English players need that much more time to adjust to the greater demands of Test cricket because the standard of county

John Crawley – found Test cricket a struggle.

cricket is lower than the Sheffield Shield. They need half a dozen Tests to get used to it.

There is also a lack of variety in county cricket these days. One of its strengths used to be that, because there were so many counties, so many players and so many different grounds, the type of cricket played would vary from match to match. Players might have to play on a dry turner at Swansea, a damp, grassy seamer at Old Trafford or a fast, bouncy wicket at the Oval. Or they might be scheduled to play during one of the festival weeks on a club pitch which would be uncovered and possibly under-prepared and bring a whole new dimension to the game.

Now we play four-day games on covered, carefully monitored pitches at fewer grounds and players go into them knowing exactly what the format is going to be. There is a dullness about it all and I would like to see more variety, more spice.

THE REMEDY

Having said all that, I don't want you to run away with the idea that everything in English cricket is wrong and the situation is beyond redemption. Far from it. We have the most professional organisation in the world. The infrastructure is first-class. And, we still have masses of talent at all levels of the game.

It is up to us to make better use of it and I think we have made a start. At the junior level, the whole business of bringing the younger players through quicker and getting them involved in international competition at an earlier age is now being co-ordinated by Micky Stewart in his role as the National Cricket Association's director of coaching. At senior level, four-day cricket, although still in its early days, is producing a higher standard of cricket than we were getting with the three-day game.

There is still a need for greater competition to stimulate players and spectators alike and I think one of the ideas that might work is to split the County Championship into two divisions with promotion and relegation at the end of the season. I know that Ray Illingworth, chairman of the England selectors, is in favour of it and I believe it has a lot of merit. You might find the better players filtering through to the bigger clubs in the 'premier league', if you like, and that might produce a bit of elitism but there is nothing wrong with that. The cricket itself would certainly maintain interest right up to the end of the season and you would not get so many of those 'dead' games which you see between middle-of-the-table sides.

In economic terms, many counties would struggle to survive without the Test and County Cricket Board's annual 'hand-out', which in 1994 was more than £700,000 per county. Whether such generosity should occur is a moot point as fewer clubs would mean fiercer competition among players.

Counties who could not maintain fully professional staffs might have to make do with semi-professionals or even let the amateurs back into the first-class game. And that might be no bad thing, either.

Not that I expect to see such radical alterations during my playing career. Fundamental change has never been the English way. We prefer to have a bit of a facelift every now and then rather than tackle the major reconstruction that might be necessary.

In any case, change like that would mean that some counties have to vote themselves out of business – and that, as the politicians say, would be like turkeys voting for Christmas.

COUNTY CHAMPIONSHIP WINNERS

County	Wins
Yorkshire	31
Surrey	18
Nottinghamshire	14
Middlesex	11
Lancashire	8
Essex	6
Kent	6
Worcestershire	5
Warwickshire	5
Gloucestershire	3
Glamorgan	2
Hampshire	2
Derbyshire	1
Leicestershire	1

- The championship has been shared by Nottinghamshire (5 times), Lancashire (4), Middlesex, Surrey, Yorkshire (2), Gloucestershire, Kent (1).
- Durham, Northamptonshire, Somerset and Sussex have never won the championship.
- Lancashire, Middlesex and Surrey have never finished bottom.

22 ONE-DAY CRICKET –
CURSE OR SALVATION?

If the County Championship is the backbone of English cricket, the one-day game is its lifeline. Without the money raised by the three domestic competitions – the NATWEST TROPHY, the BENSON AND HEDGES CUP and the AXA EQUITY AND LAW SUNDAY LEAGUE – and the one-day internationals, now sponsored by Texaco, many counties would be in a desperate financial state and some of them out of business altogether.

They were heading that way when the NatWest's predecessor, the Gillette Cup, was introduced in 1963. It was followed by the Sunday League in 1969 and the Benson and Hedges in 1972 and there can be no doubt that they have given the game a tremendous boost. Indeed if you talk to the man in the street, the bloke who is not necessarily a student of the game and neither knows nor cares too much about its intricacies, he will tell you that the *only* kind of cricket that interests him is the one-day variety.

That is almost sacrilege to those of us who have been brought up to love and understand the game of cricket but it is quite easy to see the appeal of the limited-overs stuff. For a start, it gives the spectator value for his money because he can see both sides bat and bowl and, weather permitting, get a result all in the one day. Many matches do follow a familiar pattern but it moves faster than the first-class game, there are more boundaries, more action in the field and, often, a close finish.

FOR BETTER ...

I cannot believe that the overall standard of fielding has ever been as high as it is today and one-day cricket must take a lot of the credit for that. Every player, batsman or bowler, young or old, fit or not-so-fit, practises every kind of fielding technique – close catching, deep catching, throwing, hitting the stumps, diving and stopping the ball in the outfield. You name it, they do it. Much greater emphasis has been placed on fielding because five or ten runs given away in the field can cost you a one-day match, and it must have been for the betterment of the game as a whole.

I would not say that one-day cricket has made batting standards any worse, either, although I am sure that the purists will not agree with me. Generally speaking, techniques are not as tight as they were when batsmen were brought up to play three-day and five-day cricket but they have been encouraged to play with more freedom and there is certainly more improvisation and a greater variety of shots. The reverse sweep, for example, was almost unheard of and is very much a product of the one-day game. The critics would say that is a bad thing, revealing technical frailty and making batsmen more prone to get out, but it has meant that the run-rate has improved in all forms of cricket.

The one-day game has also been a great boon to the all-rounders. Batsmen who can bowl and bowlers who can bat are of crucial importance and it cannot be a coincidence that the advent of one-day cricket led to the emergence of such great all-rounders as Ian Botham and Sir Richard Hadlee, Imran Khan and Kapil Dev.

FOR WORSE ... The bowling has certainly deteriorated. It is far more defensive as a result of one-day cricket because the emphasis is not on taking wickets but on containing the batsmen and restricting the flow of runs. We have seen the faster bowlers cutting down their pace and concentrating on bowling on one side of the wicket, much to the detriment of genuine quick bowling. But the biggest decline has been in the spin bowling. In England, at any rate, the spinners just do not spin the ball as hard as they used to do or try to turn it as much. Whereas the off-spinner would have been looking to pitch outside the off stump and turn the ball to hit it – like Australia's Tim May still does – he is now more likely to bowl at middle-and-leg with a defensive, 6–3 legside field. If you talk to John Emburey, the best English off-spinner of his time, he will admit that one-day cricket forced him to bowl more defensively and it has certainly had an adverse effect on his Test career.

RAZZMATAZZ One-day cricket is very much a product of the modern age where the demand in almost every kind of recreational activity is for more pace, more action, more colour, more excitement. As far as cricket is concerned, no country has tried harder to cater for this than Australia, who have led the way in introducing the innovations which have made one-day cricket a more and more artificial game.

On the back of Kerry Packer's revolutionary World Series Cricket which was a made-for-television spectacular, we have seen the

John Emburey – one-day cricket forced him to bowl more defensively.

introduction of the pyjama game – cricket under floodlights with coloured clothing, white balls and black sightscreens. They brought in fielding restrictions under which you can only have two players outside a thirty-yard circle in the first fifteen overs to encourage big-hitting early in an innings. They are now experimenting with a game of four quarters – one side batting for twenty-five overs, the other for twenty-five overs and then repeating the process – and they are even allowing people to play in shorts.

I am not in favour of so much artificiality but I do think there is an argument in favour of all this razzmatazz as long as it is going to finance and strengthen the more serious business of first-class cricket.

WORLD CUP WINNERS

1975	West Indies beat Australia by 17 runs	Lord's
1979	West Indies beat England by 92 runs	Lord's
1983	India beat West Indies by 43 runs	Lord's
1987	Australia beat England by 7 runs	Calcutta
1992	Pakistan beat England by 22 runs	Melbourne

ONE-DAY CHAMPIONS

	NatWest Trophy (inc Gillette Cup)	Benson and Hedges Cup	Sunday League (inc John Player, Refuge, AXA Equity & Law)
1963	Sussex	–	–
1964	Sussex	–	–
1965	Yorkshire	–	–
1966	Warwicks	–	–
1967	Kent	–	–
1968	Warwicks	–	–
1969	Yorkshire	–	Lancashire
1970	Lancashire	–	Lancashire
1971	Lancashire	–	Worcester
1972	Lancashire	Leicester	Kent
1973	Gloucester	Kent	Kent
1974	Kent	Surrey	Leicester
1975	Lancashire	Leicester	Hampshire
1976	Northants	Kent	Kent
1977	Middlesex	Gloucester	Leicester
1978	Sussex	Kent	Hampshire
1979	Somerset	Essex	Somerset
1980	Middlesex	Northants	Warwicks
1981	Derbyshire	Somerset	Essex
1982	Surrey	Somerset	Sussex
1983	Somerset	Middlesex	Yorkshire
1984	Middlesex	Lancashire	Essex
1985	Essex	Leicester	Essex
1986	Sussex	Middlesex	Hampshire
1987	Notts	Yorkshire	Worcester
1988	Middlesex	Hampshire	Worcester
1989	Warwicks	Notts	Lancashire
1990	Lancashire	Lancashire	Derbyshire
1991	Hampshire	Worcester	Notts
1992	Northants	Hampshire	Middlesex
1993	Warwicks	Derbyshire	Glamorgan
1994	Worcester	Warwicks	Warwicks
1995	Warwicks	Lancashire	Kent

In England, we have already adopted the coloured clothes and white balls in the Sunday League and I agree with reverting to a forty-over game instead of the fifty-over format which was introduced a couple of years ago. I believe Sunday should be a day out for the family to get the kids interested in cricket at an early age and it should therefore be as spectacular as possible. We should keep the coloured clothes and the white balls, keep the forty overs with a limitation on bowlers' run-ups to keep up the pace of the game and encourage batsmen to hit as many fours and sixes as possible. It is a very artificial game, compared with first-class cricket, but it is a game that youngsters enjoy watching and hopefully it will grab their interest and lead them into more sophisticated ways.

❝ *For the spectators it is a superb game. Personally I can't bear to watch it – it's too desperately stereotyped. I won a few man of the match awards but I couldn't tell you what they were.* **❞**

TED DEXTER, former England captain and chairman of selectors, on one-day cricket

RUNNING THE GAME

23 THE ADMINISTRATORS

Understanding how the game of cricket is organised and administered is not quite as simple as knowing your ABC. In fact you have to know your ICC from your TCCB, your NCA from your ESCA, and be able to tell the difference between MCC, MCCA, MCCC and a whole host of other mind-bending initials which make up a language of their own at Lord's, the headquarters of the game.

Let me try to explain.

INTERNATIONAL CRICKET COUNCIL

The International Cricket Council (ICC) is an organisation made up of all the world's cricket-playing countries and is responsible for all aspects of the international game. These include the scheduling of tours, including the World Cup, the status of Test matches, the classification of first-class games, the qualification of players, the playing conditions and regulations, the appointment of umpires, which nowadays takes in the international panel, and the appointment of match referees to oversee the new code of conduct.

Originally the 'Imperial Cricket Conference', the ICC was founded by representatives of England, Australia and South Africa at a meeting at Lord's in 1909. Membership was confined to countries within the British Commonwealth and the organisation was run by the Marylebone Cricket Club (MCC). India, New Zealand and the West Indies were elected in 1926, Pakistan in 1952, Sri Lanka in 1981 and Zimbabwe in 1992. South Africa's membership ended when they left the Commonwealth in 1961 but they were readmitted in 1991.

ICC was renamed the 'International Cricket Conference' in 1965 when new rules were adopted to allow the admission of countries from outside the Commonwealth, leading to the election of 'associate members', who have one vote compared with the full members' two, and 'affiliate members' who have no votes at all.

Clyde Walcott, chairman of the International Cricket Council.

The name was changed again to the 'International Cricket Council' in 1989 and in 1993 it set up its own independent administration at Lord's with David Richards, formerly with the Australian Cricket Board, as chief executive and Sir Clyde Walcott, the former West Indies batsman who had become one of the game's leading administrators, as the first non-British chairman.

At the last count, the membership was as follows:

FULL MEMBERS: Australia, England, India, New Zealand, Pakistan, South Africa, Sri Lanka, West Indies, Zimbabwe.

ASSOCIATE MEMBERS: Argentina, Bangladesh, Bermuda, Canada, Denmark, East and Central Africa, Fiji, Gibraltar, Hong Kong, Ireland, Israel, Kenya, Malaysia, Namibia, Netherlands, Papua New Guinea, Singapore, United Arab Emirates, USA, West Africa.

AFFILIATE MEMBERS: Austria, Bahamas, Beigium, Brunei, France, Germany, Italy, Japan, Nepal, Spain, Switzerland.

THE CRICKET COUNCIL

If you were to ask people what was the governing body for the game in the British Isles, older cricket followers would probably say MCC (the Marylebone Cricket Club) and younger ones TCCB (the Test and County Cricket Board). They would both be wrong. The supreme authority at the time of writing is the Cricket Council which was set up in 1968.

Until then, the MCC had indeed been largely responsible for running the game but under its first formal constitution the Cricket Council became the head of a new structure in which the TCCB was responsible for the administration of Test and county cricket and the National Cricket Association (NCA) for just about everything below first-class level. The MCC retained its influence as the maker and guardian of the Laws, the owner of Lord's and, as the veteran cricket writer E. W. Swanton once put it, 'guide, philosopher and friend'.

The Cricket Council is made up of eight representatives from the TCCB, five from the NCA, three from the MCC and one from the Minor Counties Cricket Association (MCCA) but all this may be about to change. By the end of 1995, the powers-that-be, recognising the need for a single body to run the game in this country, were discussing the formation of an England – or, perhaps, United Kingdom – Cricket Board.

TEST AND COUNTY CRICKET BOARD

The bosses as far as every professional cricketer in England is concerned are the TCCB. They are responsible for Test matches, tours, all first-class, Second XI and Minor Counties competitions, players' registrations, discipline, the appointment of umpires, the preparation of pitches, finance, marketing, public relations and a lot more besides.

The Board is composed of representatives of the eighteen first-class counties, MCC and MCCA, who all have a vote, and Oxford University, Cambridge University and the Irish and Scottish Cricket Unions, who do not.

From Alan (A. C.) Smith, who played Test and county cricket for England and Warwickshire and now sits behind the chief executive's desk at Lord's, to Harry Brind, who prepared some of the best pitches in the country as the Oval's groundsman and now goes around looking at everyone else's as pitches consultant, its senior employees are cricket men with a wealth of experience in the game.

Their titles and the names of the various committees, with their chairmen, explain their main functions.

Administration

Chief Executive: Alan Smith; *Cricket Secretary*: Tim Lamb; *Administrative Secretary*: Tony Brown; *Accountant*: Cliff Barker; *Marketing Manager*: Terry Blake; *Sales and Promotions*: Richard Masters; *Public Relations*: Richard Little; *England Team Manager:* Ray Illingworth.

Committees

Executive: Chairman, Dennis Silk; *Cricket*: David Acfield; *Pitches*: Donald Carr; *International*: Doug Insole; *Discipline*: Edward Slinger; *Finance*: Mike Murray; *Marketing*: Brian Downing; *Registration*: Alan Wheelhouse; *Umpires*: Alan Smith; *Second XI*: The Rev. Mike Vockins; *England Selection*: Ray Illingworth; *England Development*: Mike Smith.

COUNTY CRICKET

While the Test and County Cricket Board is predominantly composed of the eighteen first-class counties – represented by their chairman, chief executive or some other nominee – the county clubs themselves are all members' clubs, organised and run for and on behalf of the members by an elected committee.

That is the theory, anyway, although the way they do it varies considerably from county to county. They have all had their power struggles over the years and some are more democratic than others but, generally speaking, most of them are run very professionally these days with paid officials in charge of all the main areas of activity.

It is a fact of cricket life that the counties have never been able to support themselves through cricket alone. In the early days they had to rely on the patronage of the landed gentry before members' subscriptions became the major item on the profit and loss account. Even then some of them had to rely on public appeals for their existence and it is only greatly increased commercialism at all levels that has enabled them to survive as long as they have.

Warwickshire are as good an example as any of the successful, modern county club and not just because they won three of the four domestic competitions in 1994 and two in 1995. They have always been one of the more successful counties commercially – their supporters' association lent Essex the money to help them buy their Chelmsford ground in the sixties – and now operate with a high-profile chief executive in Dennis Amiss (their former England batsman), a director of coaching, a coach and manager of the indoor school, a cricket development manager, a marketing manager and an accountant. In that way, they cope with all the actual cricket, playing and coaching, from first team to schoolboy level, the administration of a major Test ground like Edgbaston, finance, sponsorship, marketing and all the ancillary activities.

All of their work will be overseen by the committee men who will have specific responsibilities in each area and will ultimately be answerable to the members for the success or failure of the club.

COUNTY MEMBERSHIP

Derbyshire	2,216	Nottinghamshire	4,362
Durham	5,448	Somerset	5,732
Essex	8,120	Surrey	5,996
Glamorgan	13,382	Sussex	5,421
Gloucestershire	4,030	Warwickshire	8,377
Hampshire	4,950	Worcestershire	4,921
Kent	5,416	Yorkshire	8,181
Lancashire	13,237	MCC	19,812
Leicestershire	4,654		
Middlesex	8,474	Total	135,258
Northamptonshire	2,526	(1994 figures)	

NATIONAL CRICKET ASSOCIATION

All English cricketers, young or old, amateur or professional, have at some time been grateful for this vast organisation which is responsible for the 'recreational' game and, crucially, the administration of the national coaching scheme.

To give you some idea of its scope, it is made up of more than fifty county cricket associations, ranging not just throughout England but from Ireland, Scotland and Wales to the Isle of Man and the Channel

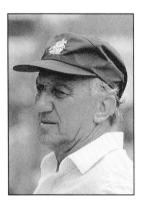

Micky Stewart –
trying to improve the
supply line.

Islands. There are also umpteen other organisations whose titles tell you about the work they do. These include:

Association of Cricket Coaches
Association of Cricket Umpires
Club Cricket Conference
Combined Services Cricket Association
Council of Cricket Societies
English Schools' Cricket Association
Headmasters' Conference Schools
Incorporated Association of Preparatory Schools
Institute of Groundsmanship
League Cricket Conference
Lord's Taverners
Midlands Club Cricket Conference
National Association of Young Cricketers
Women's Cricket Association.

Nearly 7,000 cricket clubs are also members of the NCA through their county associations; the ACC has more than 2,000 registered coaches, the ACU thousands of umpires and the schools' organisations countless budding cricketers. It is the NCA which gives them all a chance to play the game and develop their skills.

It is all run from Lord's where Terry Bates is the development and administration manager and Micky Stewart, the former England team manager, director of coaching.

His avowed intention is to improve the supply line to the England team by identifying the best young players and giving them fiercer competition at an earlier age, but he has an awesome task trying to pull together the various interests if my own experience is anything to go by. There are so many different organisations like ESCA, NAYC, NCA and MCC pulling you in so many directions that you are not sure which cap or sweater you should be wearing from one day to the next.

They all have the best intentions and, as the following list shows, they have been far from unsuccessful in producing Test players. The problem is that once our players reach that level, many of them are not as ready to cope with it as their overseas counterparts.

THE GRADUATES

Since England began playing at Under-19 level on a regular basis in 1972, nearly fifty players have 'graduated' into Test cricket. They include:

1972	Graham Gooch, Geoff Miller
1974	Nick Cook, Chris Cowdrey, Mike Gatting, Vic Marks, Graham Stevenson, Chris Tavare
1976	Paul Allott, Bill Athey, Paul Downton, David Gower
1977	Tony Pigott, Jack Richards, Paul Terry
1978	Graham Dilley, Richard Ellison, Bruce French
1979	Jonathan Agnew, Kim Barnett, Norman Cowans, Neil Foster
1980	Neil Mallender
1981	David Lawrence
1982	Robert Bailey, David Capel, Richard Illingworth, Paul Jarvis, Hugh Morris, Jack Russell
1983	John Morris, Neil Fairbrother, Steve Rhodes, Peter Such
1985	Richard Blakey, Phillip DeFreitas, Phil Tufnell
1986	Martin Bicknell, Angus Fraser, Mark Ramprakash
1987	Mike Atherton, Nasser Hussain, Chris Lewis
1988	Peter Martin
1989	Graham Thorpe, Dominic Cork, Darren Gough
1990	John Crawley
1991	Mark Lathwell

SPIRIT OF THE GAME

24 CONDUCT – BECOMING OR OTHERWISE?

In October 1991, the International Cricket Council drew up a Code of Conduct and introduced match referees for all Tests and one-day internationals. This is how Sir Colin Cowdrey, then chairman of ICC, explained the move:

The game of cricket throughout the world flourishes and more people are playing than ever before. This is largely due to the media, be it newspaper coverage and the journals, the radio or, in recent years, television with its miracle eye and instant replays, bringing every detail of the game into the home with the mysteries clearly revealed. It is this that has captured the imagination of a huge new cricket following.

Test cricketers today live under the intensity of this spotlight and carry with them an unenviable burden of responsibility.

Without undermining in any way the compelling ingredients of fierce combat where all the skills are deployed in pursuit of victory, the players must maintain the highest standards of conduct on the field.

It is to preserve the image of the game and the players' profession that a Match Referee will be in place at all Test matches to support the umpire. A Code of Conduct has been drawn up as a guideline to captain, player, match referee and umpire.

The focus of attention is directed towards the captain emphasising his responsibility under the Laws of the Game that at all times he should see that his players conduct themselves within the Spirit of the Game as well as within the Laws of the Game.

It is the duty of every player, as he walks out from the shade of the pavilion, to be aware of his responsibility to both his captain and the game and to set his own standard of self-discipline.

Cricket has no place for the cheat, the foul-mouthed or for those who deal in verbal abuse and, worst of all, those who fail to show proper respect for the umpire's authority.

Sixty years ago, Lord Harris implored all cricketers 'to play the game keenly, honourably, generously and self-sacrificingly' and that 'we should protect it from anything that would sully it, so that it may be in favour with all men.'

The game is always changing, yet these words, and their sentiments, stand the test of the time.

THE CODE

1. The captains are responsible at all times for ensuring that play is conducted within the spirit of the game as well as within the Laws.
2. Players and team officials shall not at any time engage in conduct unbecoming to an international player or team official which could bring them or the game into disrepute.
3. Players and team officials must at all times accept the umpire's decision. Players must not show dissent at the umpire's decision.
4. Players and team officials shall not intimidate, assault or attempt to intimidate or assault an umpire, another player or a spectator.
5. Players and team officials shall not use crude or abusive language (known as 'sledging') nor make offensive gestures.
6. Players and team officials shall not use or in any way be concerned in the use or distribution of illegal drugs.
7. Players and team officials shall not disclose or comment upon any alleged breach of the Code or upon any hearing, report or decision arising from such breach.
8. Players and team officials shall not make any public pronouncement or media comment which is detrimental either to the game in general or to a particular tour in which they are involved, or about any tour between other countries which is taking place, or to relations between the boards of the competing teams.

I have no quarrel with any of that. The umpires are there to make sure that the game is conducted properly; they have the match referees to back them up and the players respect their authority. But I have to say that, in certain cases, they have not been as strong as they might be – and especially when it comes to clamping down on intimidatory bowling.

It is quite right for the match referee to keep a low profile in a good-tempered, well-behaved Test match and let everyone get on with the game. But when players exceed what is generally regarded as acceptable, the referees should step in and do something about it

– and when they do step in, they should be more consistent in the judgments they make and the penalties they impose.

What is unacceptable is any form of dissent against the umpire's decision. All cricketers still regard that as final, sacrosanct, the be-all and end-all of everything that happens on a cricket pitch.

It was UNACCEPTABLE for the England captain, Mike Gatting, to argue with umpire Shakoor Rana during the 1987 tour of Pakistan; UNACCEPTABLE for Chris Broad to stand there and refuse to leave the crease after being given out; UNACCEPTABLE for me to argue with umpires Darrell Hair and Lloyd Barker in the heat of the moment during the 1994 Barbados Test following a strange decision while we were in the field.

It must be remembered, however, that Test matches are emotional occasions and players under pressure cannot be expected to behave like robots.

Merv Hughes gives Alec Stewart the treatment.

No hard feelings. Malcolm Marshall welcomes Mike Gatting back to the Caribbean after breaking his nose in 1986.

You do get the occasional unsavoury incident but I can honestly say that all the series I have played in for England have been contested in a really good spirit. Certainly in the six we played between 1994 and 1996 – against the West Indies, New Zealand, South Africa, and Australia – the cricket was hard but it was fair. There is not so much socialising between the teams as there used to be and we do not go into each other's dressing rooms for a beer at close of play but we do try to have a drink together at the end of a series.

Generally speaking, most of the sides do get on well and sometimes you find a couple of cricketers becoming very good friends. In Australia, for example, Darren Gough and Shane Warne, two talented players with fairly similar personalities, got on together like a house on fire. They are kindred spirits, if you like, with a happy-go-lucky outlook on life and they seemed to hit it off from the start.

❝ It was a funny thing to call yourself. ❞

New Zealand's MARTIN CROWE in answer to Aqib's defence that he was talking to himself when he called the umpire 'a f***ing cheat'

DOUBLE TROUBLE

Pakistan fast bowler Aqib Javed completed a unique double in 1992 when he became the first player to be both fined and banned by match referees under the Code of Conduct. He was fined £250 by Conrad Hunte for 'petulant behaviour' after being warned for intimidatory bowling by umpire Roy Palmer at Old Trafford and suspended for one match by Peter Burge for 'obscene abuse' of umpire Brian Aldridge in New Zealand.

INTERNATIONAL PANEL OF UMPIRES

❝ The modern umpire is caught between two opposing forces – the domestic pressures which encourage errors and the technology which reveals them. ❞

Former Pakistan captain IMRAN KHAN

In 1994, the International Cricket Council introduced an international panel of umpires paid for by a £1·1m sponsorship over three years by National Grid. Each Test-playing country nominated two umpires – apart from England who named four because a) they have more than anybody else and b) most Test matches are played during the English winter. A 'neutral' umpire would stand with a 'home' umpire in every Test and countries would have no right of objection to any appointment.

I agree with the policy in principle and think that the system is working very well although I would prefer to have two 'neutral' umpires if the funding was available. I also think it is important to have umpires who do the job on a fulltime basis. For example, Jamaica's Steve Bucknor is virtually a professional umpire and has done an excellent job everywhere he has been.

Where I disagree with the present system is in the policy of having a third umpire sitting in the pavilion watching television replays to adjudicate on line decisions – and the practice in South Africa of using red and green lights to signal whether a batsman is out or not out.

There have been a number of instances where the television cameras have been unable to provide a satisfactory replay because they are in the wrong place or a batsman or fielder has obscured the line or the stumps and I do not think that this is acceptable. I also think that the third umpire has sometimes made a hasty decision when he has all the time he needs to study the replays and got it wrong himself.

And I am definitely against the use of lights to indicate the verdict. I like to see the umpire making the decision in the time-honoured way.

I accept – and I'm sure we all accept – that umpires are human beings and they are going to make mistakes just as batsmen, bowlers, fielders and, of course, captains, make mistakes. And I want to keep that human element in the game.

A final thought is that if the technology is to be used, then it should be used consistently. In Australia in 1994–5 we had a situation where two crucial run outs were not given because the umpire did not ask for a replay. And in South Africa in 1995–6, their captain, Hansie Cronje, had to persuade the umpire, Dave Orchard, to call for a replay after the crowd's reaction told him that television had shown he had got it wrong. While I would not want to blame Hansie for asking for the replay, it was wrong for an umpire's decision to be changed in this way. Captains are specifically told by match referees not to ask for a replay, which is why Hansie was fined fifty per cent of his match fee. But if the technology is there, umpires should use it.

25 PROFESSIONALISM

As far as cricket is concerned, the distinction between the amateur and the professional, or the 'gentlemen' and the 'players' as they were called, was abolished in 1962. The basic difference, of course, was one of payment although there was much talk of 'shamateurism' – the practice whereby some of the gentlemen were actually being paid more than the players through appointments with their counties, sponsorship or jobs which depended on their names and allowed them plenty of time off to play cricket. And when it came to 'professionalism', some of the amateurs knew far more about it than the professionals did.

We are all players now and that does make a difference to our attitude to the game. Inherent in this is the inescapable fact that cricket is a sport, a pastime, which we all took up in the first place because we enjoyed playing the game and because it was fun. Once you become a professional, it becomes a job, a livelihood, and everything takes on a more serious bent. Sometimes you forget that playing cricket is supposed to be an enjoyable experience. For the amateur it is not like that. The fun side of the game remains.

For me, the difference between amateurs and professionals falls into three categories – the obvious one of payment, the amount of time spent working at the game and the gamesmanship and all that kind of stuff which has tended to make 'professionalism' a dirty word.

Payment

In England, professionals are paid a six-month salary by their county clubs and, if they are good enough to play international cricket, a further six-month salary by the TCCB for going on tour. In Australia, for example, the system is different. There, the Test players are contracted to the Australian Cricket Board on a year-round salary while the state players are more semi-professional with other jobs on the side.

Work

Professionalism also means that cricket becomes a more serious pursuit with players spending much more time training, practising and studying videos of themselves to try to improve all aspects of their game.

Professionalism implies people at the top of their game working as hard as they possibly can to to be the best they possibly can. Certainly under Graham Gooch's captaincy, the England side took on a more professional outlook compared with what had gone before. Under Graham and team manager Micky Stewart, the England players trained harder and practised harder in an attempt to produce a thoroughly professional outfit which should be the minimum requirement for a sportsman representing his country.

Gamesmanship

To some people, this is just another word for professionalism but when it comes down to it there is not that much difference between the professionals and the amateurs. Indeed, in my experience, League cricket in the north of England is sometimes much worse than first-class cricket in terms of gamesmanship, sledging and the spirit between the sides.

❝ After I had been batting a short while, Godfrey Evans said to me: 'Before you came in, I knew you were no gentleman. Now that I've seen you batting a bit, I realise that you're not a player, either. **❞**

RAMAN SUBBA ROW, former England batsman, recalling the 1958 Gentlemen v. Players match at Lord's

❝ All the Gentlemen should be players and all the Players gentlemen. **❞**

ALBERT CRAIG, poet

KITTED OUT

26 THE BAT

Cricket bats have evolved over the years from simple staves hacked from trees and hedgerows to bulbous wooden clubs, from curved implements shaped like hockey sticks to the scientifically designed precision instruments you see today. They have progressed from solid lumps of timber which jarred the hands when you struck the ball and left the fingers tingling, into beautifully hand-crafted tools with springy handles and so-called 'sweet spots' which cushion the ball on impact.

There are five major manufacturers of cricket bats in England – Duncan Fearnley, Gray-Nicolls, Gunn & Moore, Slazenger and Stuart Surridge – with others such as Centurion, Kookaburra and Open Championship entering the market from time to time. The newcomers are good news for the professionals because 'the big five' operate a kind of cartel with an agreement not to pay players more than a certain amount for using their brands so when a new firm starts waving its cheque book the slice of cake goes a little bit further.

There is not that much money around in cricket and bat sponsorship is one area in which the top players look for a reasonable deal. A Test batsman playing regularly in international cricket would expect upwards of £20,000 per calendar year.

I use a Gray-Nicolls bat and always have done since I became a professional cricketer. I like to think that I have been loyal to the company and that they have been loyal to me but you do find some players who have been connected with five or six different firms during their careers. When we met up at Heathrow before the last tour of Australia, Phil Tufnell and Devon Malcolm were busy finalising their latest bat deals with Centurion. I would have thought they would have been better off paying those two not to use them – although the change of company has obviously worked wonders for Devon, who smashed his highest Test score of 29 in the 1995 Sydney Test.

With plenty of competition around, the bat-makers are always coming up with new ideas, which are sometimes not much more than gimmicks, but there have been many important developments which have improved the batsman's lot – and made life a lot harder for the bowlers.

The most obvious of these has been the trend towards heavier bats, pioneered by Tony Greig, who was probably the first to use a three-pounder, and taken up by many of the more powerful stroke-makers like Clive Lloyd, Graham Gooch and Graeme Hick. There is no doubt that this has taken a heavy toll of the spinner on the smaller grounds.

I remember ribbing Graham Gooch about this, saying that I thought it was more of a challenge to use a light bat because you had to hit the sweet spot to get the ball away. He replied in that eminently practical way of his, pointing out that a heavy bat does not actually give you a better sweet spot but it certainly gives you a bigger one. You could therefore mistime a shot and it would still go for six. I suppose it would – in his case.

Generally speaking, heavy bats tend to be for the firm-wristed players, the big drivers like Gooch and Hick; light bats for the more wristy, touch players like India's captain Mohammad Azharuddin. Azza's bat weighs around 2lb 4oz and is probably the lightest I have picked up.

The exception is little Sachin Tendulkar who defies all the advice, going back to W. G. Grace's day, that batsmen should not use bats that are too big for them, by using one which is very weighty for his size. And he is quite a wristy player as well.

It is important to remember that he is an exception, though. When a boy goes with his parents to buy a bat, his dad will often choose one that is too big and too heavy for him on the grounds that he is still growing. But it is of paramount importance for a youngster to have a bat which is the right length and the right height for him. Using a bat that is too big or too heavy can lead to flaws in your technical play.

My bats are around 2lb 7oz, which is regarded as fairly average, although we don't actually weigh them. I generally go to the Gray-Nicolls factory and get the bat-maker to pick out seven or eight bats which he thinks are reasonable bits of wood and I will select what I consider to be the best four. I might get him to shave a bit off to change the balance slightly but I don't go by the scales but by the feel and the pick-up which can sometimes be very different to the actual weight.

How many bats you need in a year probably does depend on the

India's captain, Mohammad Azharuddin, still packs plenty of power with one of the lightest bats in world cricket.

weight and, because mine are quite light, I will get through two or three. I like to have three on the go at any one time – one, my 'best' bat, which I try to keep for Test matches and other big games, one for the other matches, and one that I am 'knocking in' in the nets.

Bat handles tend to be too thin for my liking and I generally have two rubbers around the handle. Most batsmen will have more than one to give them a better 'feel' in the hands although some, like Nasser Hussain, actually like a very thin grip. At the other end of the scale, Clive Lloyd had a legendary bat, weighing over 3lb with five or six rubbers around the handle.

There have been other famous – and some quite infamous – bats. Gray-Nicolls introduced the 'scoop' bat which had one, two or even four scoops at the back to spread the weight across the middle of the bat and give it a larger sweet spot. I played golf once with the chap who developed the idea from the parameter weighted golf club.

There have been bats with no shoulders, as used by New Zealand's Lance Cairns, and bats with replaceable edges. Dennis Lillee even held up a Test match by going out to bat with an aluminium bat. Mike Brearley, then England's captain, objected on the grounds that it might damage the ball and there was a long delay before Lillee's captain, Greg Chappell, threw the strange, shiny object away and told him to get on with the game – with a decent piece of willow.

27 GLOVES

Gloves, like bats, have come a long way over the years – from the open-palmed wraparound variety with straps around the wrist, to flimsy cotton things with green rubber spikes on the back, to full-fronted mittens like boxing gloves which Tony Greig used to wear.

Most players have now gone back to the 'sausage' type of glove or even the 'double sausage' with extra protection for the two forefingers. But there is still room for improvement.

Despite all the modifications, the number of broken fingers suffered by batsmen is still increasing which suggests to me that the standard of fast bowling – and the amount of it – has risen more significantly than the quality of batting gloves.

I get through a lot of gloves for the simple reason that I like wearing new ones. I like the feel of them on the bat and before every match I will put a new rubber on the bat handle and look for the freshest pair of gloves I can find. Because of this I will take ten or a dozen pairs with me when I go on tour.

Robin Smith is even more particular, going through hundreds of pairs, yet some batsmen are quite the opposite. Graham Saville, the former Essex batsman who managed the England Under-19 side, told me that he hated changing his gloves and preferred batting in an old sweaty pair.

The main reason for changing them frequently is the obvious one – because they get very sweaty, particularly in hot, humid climates like Guyana or Sri Lanka. You can get through two or three pairs in one innings if you are lucky enough to bat for that long.

Changing batting gloves is also a tactical ploy when a captain wants to get a message out to one of his batsmen because he wants to push the score along or he is thinking about a declaration. Then you will see the captain trying to attract the batsman's attention and the twelfth man trotting out with a fresh pair of gloves – whether he wants them or not.

28 ALL THAT PADDING

The increase in the volume and the pace of fast bowling has naturally increased the amount of protective padding that batsmen wear over and above – and underneath – the familiar PADS. These are normally made on the Sub-Continent and you are obviously looking for maximum protection coupled with maximum comfort. I will try a different pair at the start of each English season and the beginning of each tour and I hope that they last the distance.

I wear two THIGH PADS, one on the outside of the left thigh, the other towards the inside of the right thigh. Theoretically, the one on the right should not be needed because if you stay sideways-on as the text book says, you should not get hit there. Unfortunately no one has told the bowlers that and you lose count of the number of times you are turned square and the ball hits the inside of that right thigh. Another important factor is that when the ball does strike your thigh and you set off for a run you can easily pull a muscle so you need some protection to prevent that kind of injury.

Even Ian Botham needed a helmet, a chest protector and an arm guard when he was facing the West Indies.

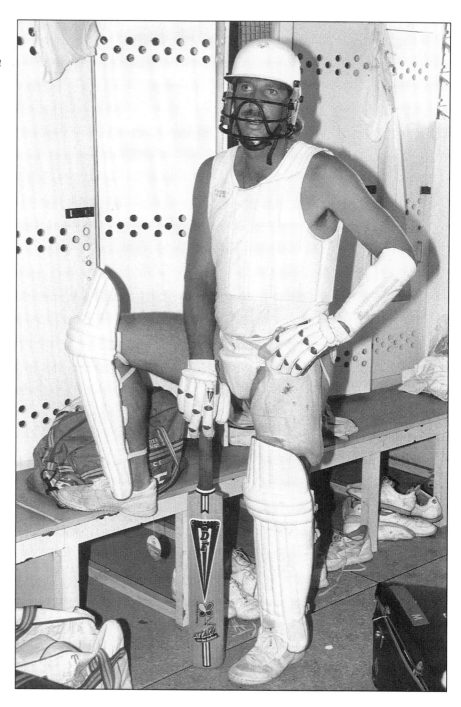

Australia's Mark Waugh has another use for his thigh pad. Every time he scores a first-class century he puts a little sticker on it and he now has more than forty of them.

The CHEST PROTECTOR – one type is like chainmail and pulled

on over the head, others are strapped on to cover the ribcage – has become a vital part of a batsman's equipment in recent years although I had never worn one myself until we went to the West Indies in 1994.

I decided to have one 'made to measure' and shaped to fit my ribcage and it came in very useful in Jamaica and Antigua where I was twice hit in the ribs. Each time the ball cannoned safely off the padding and once I am sure it also saved my wicket. I got a short, lifting ball and was able to raise my arms and let the ball hit me in the chest when otherwise I might have flinched and 'gloved' a catch to the wicketkeeper.

The forearm is another vulnerable area when you are facing a lot of fast bowling and many batsmen now wear an ARM GUARD which is taped to the left forearm if you are a right-hander. I usually wear one on quick wickets but not always. It depends how I feel on the day.

Finally we must not forget the BOX, or abdominal protector, to give it its proper name, which can be crucial to a batsman's well-being for fairly obvious reasons. It is hard to explain why it should cause so much hilarity when a batsman is hit in such a painful place but there are times when you just cannot help laughing … unless you are the player involved.

David Lloyd tells how he was struck a particularly devastating blow by Jeff Thomson on England's tour of Australia in 1974–5. It smashed his box to smithereens and he fell, unconscious, head-first on to the bone-hard Perth pitch. When he came round he was not sure what had suffered the most damage – his nose or another part of his anatomy.

What is beyond dispute is that you often need every bit of that padding – and sometimes more. Devon Malcolm's idiosyncratic batting technique meant that when Courtney Walsh was giving him a going over he kept being hit up the backside. Darren Gough went out to bat against Alan Donald at Lord's with a guard on his left arm and was hit on his *right*. And Jack Russell takes no chances at all. He has a bit of padding for every part of his body and when he has got it all on it looks like a suit of armour.

29 HELMETS

Dennis Amiss, the former England and Warwickshire opening batsman, came in for a lot of ribbing when, in the aftermath of his battering by Lillee and Thomson on the 1974–5 tour of Australia, he designed what looked like a motorcyclist's crash helmet. No one ribs him now because there is absolutely no doubt that the introduction of the batting helmet has since saved many lives.

There was a lot of experimentation before we arrived at the neat, compact model we have today. Mike Brearley and Sunil Gavaskar wore their protection underneath their caps or floppy hats, with flaps covering the temples which are a particularly vulnerable part of the head. We had perspex visors before the present detachable metal grilles and it looked as though we were going full circle when Matthew Maynard sported a motorbike style of helmet on England's last tour of the West Indies.

They tell me it is very safe but it would have to be since every kind of helmet has to be passed by the British Standards Institute which makes sure that they come up to the required safety standard.

For

The case for helmets is obvious. Batsmen wear them for protection. New Zealand's Ewan Chatfield was not wearing one when he was struck on the temple by Peter Lever at Auckland in 1975 and only the prompt action of England's physiotherapist, Bernard Thomas, saved his life. South Africa's Jonty Rhodes was wearing one when he was struck on the temple by Devon Malcolm at the Oval in 1994 and I am sure he would have been killed but for the helmet. As it was, he had to spend a night in hospital and was back on the field the next day.

For my own part, I am convinced that I would have suffered a broken jaw when I was hit by Winston Benjamin if I had not been properly protected.

The helmet also provides protection for fielders at silly point and short leg and though some people think they should not be there if they are not prepared to take their chances I see nothing wrong with it. I remember seeing Lancashire against Derbyshire when Steve Jeffries was swinging the ball in and wanted a man at short leg.

Lancashire's captain, John Abrahams, went there for the last ball of the over and, sure enough, Kim Barnett immediately clipped a half volley straight into his mouth. A new set of teeth was required.

Against

The one valid argument against helmets is that players tend to lose their identity when they are wearing them. Denis Compton, who played long before they were introduced and probably wouldn't have worn one anyway, said that he did not like them precisely because the spectators could not feel one-to-one with their particular favourites.

Maybe he has a point but all the other arguments against helmets are absolute rubbish. It is just not true to say, as some people do, that batsmen lose that sixth sense, feeling that because they are wearing helmets they can let the ball hit them. You don't think like that all. You damned well do try to get out of the way because the ball still hurts.

It is a fact, I'm afraid, that the number and variety of the fast bowlers, the fierceness of their deliveries and the unpredictability of the pitches have all increased over the years so that the case for helmets is stronger than it ever was. Alan Knott tells me that if he faced four bouncers in a season of championship cricket in the sixties it was a bad year. In any case, the pitches were more even then so that when the ball was dug in short you could duck with confidence. That is not the case today.

Some batsmen even keep their helmets on against the spinners and there are good reasons for that, too. Some spinners can be quite quick and bouncy when they want to be and, whatever their pace, there is always the danger of a top edge into the face when you are trying to sweep them on a turning wicket. And, invariably, it is just after you have taken your helmet off that the nasty blow comes.

❝ If someone had produced a batting helmet during the Bodyline series, I would certainly have worn it. ❞

SIR DONALD BRADMAN

❝ I don't know what the game's coming to. You wouldn't get me wearing one of those plastic things. ❞

BRIAN CLOSE

---

30 BOOTS

The right kind of footwear is obviously essential to any self-respecting cricketer. Naturally you want to be comfortable whether you are batting, bowling or fielding but there is more to it than that.

I always carry three pairs of boots around with me – one pair of full spikes, one pair with rubber soles and one pair that are half and half.

Bowlers *always* wear full spikes because they never know when the captain is going to ask them to bowl. They have to be ready to come charging in whether the ground is hard and dry or soft and slippery and it would be dangerous for them not to be properly shod.

Bowling is also very hard on the feet, especially for the fast bowlers, and they will go to great lengths to make sure their boots are tough enough to take the constant pounding yet at the same time comfortable enough to spend a day in the field. Angus Fraser, for example, will spend up to £200 to have boots specially made for his enormous feet.

Bowlers also suffer from sore toes, especially those who drag the back foot, and will have steel toe caps fitted for extra protection. Derek Pringle, typically, went the other way and cut a hole in his toe cap to ease the pressure. It became such a trademark that he even incorporated a boot with a hole in it on his benefit tie.

As captain, I also ask the fielders to wear full spikes as well because there is nothing worse than missing catches or giving away runs in the field just because you are wearing the wrong footwear. I learned this lesson very early in my career when I fielded in rubbers in a Sunday League match against Middlesex at Lord's and found myself slipping and sliding all over the place. David Hughes, the Lancashire captain, gave me one of the biggest rollickings of my life and I have fielded in full spikes ever since.

Batsmen generally wear what they feel most comfortable in, some, like Graham Gooch, preferring full spikes, others, like Robin Smith, rubbers.

I choose to bat in half-spiked boots even though this did cost me

KITTED OUT – BOOTS

dearly when I was run out for 99 against Australia at Lord's in 1993. I was running on the lush, green grass at the side of the pitch when I went to turn with the heel, the rubber part of the sole, on the turf and slipped. I was run out in some embarrassment but I have not heeded that lesson. I just feel more comfortable in those kinds of boots.

31 A GENTLEMAN'S ACCESSORIES

So far we have discussed the essential items of a cricketer's equipment. But what are we to make of the other accessories like designer sunglasses, Walkmans, mobile phones, sun blocks and sponsored cars, most of them supplied with the help of an agent working on the players' behalf? I can almost hear the old-timers wondering what the game is coming to.

We have certainly come a long way since Denis Compton's Brylcreemed hair gleamed from the advertising hoardings and the sides of London buses but it is no more than a natural progression in these highly commercial times.

Most players carry a pair of SUNGLASSES around with them and that is hardly surprising when you consider some of the places they have to play in. The light in countries like Australia, India and throughout the Caribbean can be quite dazzling although I have only once worn my shades on the field. That was in Bombay when the sun was very low and I was fielding in the deep and since I actually took two catches I was very grateful for them.

There are times, though, when they are not absolutely necessary and it is true that certain players wear them for non-cricketing reasons – like fashion and, in some cases, payment.

The same goes for SUN BLOCK which is just as necessary as sunglasses in countries where there is real concern about skin cancer and players are advised to protect themselves from the sun as much as possible.

Cricketers are not alone in carrying a WALKMAN and their own choice of music with them as they travel around the world and they can be very useful either for relaxation purposes or for providing an up-beat atmosphere in the dressing room. Players like Graham Gooch and Devon Malcolm invariably have their headphones on before they go out to bat or bowl. Goochy will be listening to something stirring. Devon is more likely to choose a bit of Bob Marley.

There has been a lot of nonsense talked about MOBILE PHONES in the England dressing room – ranging from the notion that the players spend most of their time using them, to the idea that they have been banned altogether. The fact of the matter is that we do not encourage their use during the hours of play. Many of the players do have their own phones but they do not use them quite as much as Allan Lamb who seemed to spend most of one series with one at each ear.

Many counties do provide SPONSORED CARS which is not altogether surprising considering the amount of travelling players have to do during an English season but they are a lot harder to come by than they used to be. A few years ago Lancashire had about fourteen cars supplied by Rover but they were down to three in 1994. Most of the international players will have one, though, and I am fortunate enough to have a Peugeot, sponsored by Tom Garner, a local garage.

Most of these commercial deals are negotiated by agents who are an accepted part of a professional sportsman's life these days. Some are good, some not so good, and though I may be biased I think that my own agent, Jon Holmes, is better than most and the acceptable face of the sportsman's agent.

There are some sharks around and you have to find someone who you can trust but anyone who believes that a top player can manage without an agent has only got to look at the amount of hype that surrounded Brian Lara after his phenomenal performances in 1994. He must have had offers coming at him from all directions so you can understand why he needed a good agent. Similarly, the amount of adulation heaped upon Darren Gough on his return to England in 1995 will have brought home to him, if he did not know already, that he is in some ways public property now. However much people argue against it, he needs – and indeed has found – a good agent, so he can remain focused on the main job at hand, his success on the cricket field.

> **66** McDermott will never be as good a bowler as Miller and Lindwall so long as he bowls in a watch. **99**
>
> JOHN WOODCOCK, *Times* cricket writer

Cricketers used to carry their gear around in cricket bags. Today we have enormous cases which we call 'coffins'. To help you understand why, these are the contents of mine, although I've probably forgotten something!

Bats (3/4)
Boots (3 pairs)
Trousers (2)
Shirts (3)
Sweaters (2)
Socks (3)
Gloves (4/5)
Pads (1 pair)
Thigh pads (2)

Chest protector (1)
Arm guard (1)
Box (1)
Helmet and grille (1)
Cap
Sun hat
Sunglasses
Zinc cream
Fly spray

Sweat bands
Bat grips
Bat tape
Coloured clothing
    for Sunday
    League or one-day
    internationals.

If you think that's a lot, Jack Russell has two coffins. Wicketkeepers do have more gear but he is perhaps more eccentric than most.

PUBSPEAK

32 THE TROUBLE WITH CRICKET IS …

I like a pint of decent beer but I am not in the habit of getting involved in the kind of arguments which gain momentum in ratio to the amount of ale that is consumed whenever two or three cricket fanatics are gathered at the bar. I do know what they are talking about, though, and this is my chance to contribute to the 'discussions' which invariably start: 'The trouble with cricket is …'

'Too many foreigners play for England'

It depends what you mean by foreigners. There are players who were born in England (or the United Kingdom, which means the same when it comes to cricket) but brought up elsewhere; players who were brought up in England but born elsewhere; and players who do not have much connection with England at all apart from a residential qualification.

It is a very complex question but a distinction you could make, I suppose, is between those players who came to England to live and those who came to play cricket.

Take the cases of Martin McCague and Craig White, who both played for England on the 1994–5 tour of Australia. They were both born in the UK – Martin in Northern Ireland, Craig in Yorkshire – but were taken to Australia when they were very young. They were brought up there and actually learned their cricket there but then came back to live in England in order to pursue their professional careers.

When it came to playing Test cricket, they were qualified to play for England by birth or for Australia by residence and we are delighted that they chose to play for us.

They are a quite different case from someone like their latest England colleague, Joey Benjamin, who was born on the Caribbean island of St Kitts but was brought to England by his parents as a boy. It was then that he took up cricket, eventually becoming good enough to represent Warwickshire and Surrey and, proudly, England.

A player like Graeme Hick is different again. He decided he wanted to play for England before his native Zimbabwe were granted Test status and spent seven years with Worcestershire qualifying to do so. He is now a naturalised Englishman and, as such, he has an unalienable right to play for England.

I can certainly understand the layman's view because, as a proud Englishman myself, I think we would all like to see eleven Englishmen playing for England. But I have played for England with many players like Robin Smith and Graeme Hick and I can honestly say that it has been an absolute honour. They give nothing less than their best whenever they pull on that England sweater with the three lions and the crown.

Having said that, I will concede that qualification is a problem in this ever-shrinking world. I am pleased that the ICC and the TCCB have been tightening up on the Regulations to prevent players abusing the system if they have no intention of declaring a desire to play for the country.

'The selectors do not watch enough cricket'

If this ever was the case, it is certainly not the case now. In 1994, the England selectors were Keith Fletcher, Brian Bolus and Fred Titmus under the chairmanship of Ray Illingworth and they were out watching county cricket almost every day of the week.

Robin Smith – never gives less than 100 per cent for England.

*With Ray
Illingworth, a
professional northern
cricketer – like me!*

At the start of his tenure, Illy wrote down the names of fifty players who had a chance of playing for England and they were watched very closely. Every county was visited a number of times and every player who was in contention for an England place could have come under the selectors' scrutiny at some stage.

The proposition may have been true in the past. Ian Botham likes to joke about 'the gin and tonic set', explaining that the selectors watch their cricket through the bottom of a glass. But I can assure you that today's selectors take their duties very seriously and regard their jobs as a profession in the same way as the players do.

'There just isn't enough cricket played in schools'

This one is definitely true, I'm afraid. There has been a sad decline in the amount of cricket played in schools even since my schooldays which were not all that long ago. I suppose it came on the back of the teachers' strike in the early eighties and they do not give nearly as much time to cricket as they used to do, especially in state schools.

Public schools still have a decent amount of cricket, which may have something to do with the fact that they are better able to afford what is, after all, an expensive game. You need plenty of money to buy bats and pads and all the other equipment. You also need good facilities – certainly either a turf pitch or an artificial one – and many state schools just cannot afford them.

There is a need for a good proportion of the £60 million which the Test and County Cricket Board is receiving from its latest television deal to go into the grass roots of the game, because unless there is an improvement at that level the supply of players to first-class cricket is going to be limited. In many areas, it is being left to the clubs to take up the slack. In the north, we have a strong League structure and it is up to the clubs to take the boys on and give them the opportunities they need.

'They spend too much time on fitness training and not enough in the nets'

Nine-tenths of the England team's 'training time' *is* spent in the nets, working on technique and practising.

All the nonsense talked about an over-emphasis on fitness training arose during Graham Gooch's period as captain yet all he was saying was that there was a need for England to be more professional. He could see that other countries had become much more professional than we were and he recognised the need for us to catch up.

The fact was that he had taken over the captaincy from David Gower, who had been very laid back about it all. The difference between the Gower and the Gooch regimes was accentuated by the somewhat casual approach of one and the ultra-professionalism of the other and the contrast was very stark. But some of the allegations, like saying that players were going on five-mile runs and tiring themselves out before matches, were blatant rubbish.

There was a need for a balance between the two extremes and

what I have tried to do is strike it somewhere in the middle. We concentrate mainly on cricket skills and incorporate a certain amount of fitness training into our fielding practice, hopefully killing two birds with one stone.

In any case, fitness for cricket is a specialised subject. You obviously need to be fit to play the game but it is a different kind of fitness to what you need for other sports. To put cricketers through the same kind of training schedule as footballers and rugby players, for instance, is stupid, in my view. Such sports make completely different demands. Ask a cricketer to go into a rugby scrum and he would struggle. Ask a footballer or a rugby player to stand for six hours in the field in Sri Lanka and I can tell you he would struggle as well.

The problem for England players derives from the fact that we play so much. We have our county commitments in between the Test and international matches and any days off are needed for rest. As any fitness expert will tell you, rest is an important part of fitness. Consider an England cricketer's schedule in 1995–6:

May–Aug	Six Tests plus three one-day internationals in England.
Oct–Jan	Five Tests plus seven one-day internationals in South Africa.
Feb–March	World Cup in India, Pakistan and Sri Lanka.
May–Sept	Six Tests and six one-day internationals in England.

County commitments on top of that left little time for extracurricular fitness programmes.

'It's all about money, money, money'

Well, money is an important factor in any professional sportsman's career – and especially a cricketer's. It is only a short career, particularly at international level, and you have to capitalise on it.

Cricket is very much the poor relation when it comes to international sport with even the greatest players earning only a fraction of what the stars of football and golf, athletics and motor racing, baseball and basketball are getting. Cricketers work just as hard as many of them do, playing six or seven days a week for ten months of the year, and they deserve some material reward.

There is very little money in county cricket, anyway, with the average player picking up around £15,000 or £16,000 a year. If he is lucky enough to go on to play at international level, he will earn upwards of £80,000 including advertising, sponsorship, etc. The difference is massive and you cannot blame players for trying to make the most of it through advertising, television appearances, bat contracts and the like.

WHAT THEY EARN

Britain's highest-paid sportsmen in 1993 with estimated earnings.

Lennox Lewis	Boxer	£10.5m
Nigel Mansell	Racing driver	£7.5m
Nick Faldo	Golfer	£7m
Paul Gascoigne	Footballer	£2.9m
Nigel Benn	Boxer	£2.4m
Ian Woosnam	Golfer	£2.2m
Gary Lineker	Footballer	£2.1m
Colin Montgomerie	Golfer	£1.9m
David Platt	Footballer	£1.5m
Stephen Hendry	Snooker player	£1.4m

A top cricketer like Graham Gooch would not have earned more than £100,000.

But to say that cricket is *all* about money is just not true. There are a number of reasons for playing and first and foremost is that love of the game which attracted us to it in the first place. Once you start to play, you obviously want to do the best you can in terms of honours won and caps received, coupled with the natural desire to play for one's country.

As far as I am concerned, that is the greatest motivation of all and I can assure you that when I am playing for England money is the last thing on my mind.

'Today's players won't listen to the "greats" of the game'

This one is only half true. Some players do listen; some don't listen quite as much.

My attitude is that I don't want to listen to everybody because if you listen to too many people you finish up with so much advice that it becomes confusing.

If there is good advice around, then I'm only too ready to listen. I spent a lot of time under the tutelage of Geoff Boycott before I went to Zimbabwe with England 'A' in the winter of 1989 and I found his advice about Test cricket very useful indeed from both a technical and a mental point of view. He has been a confidant as regards how I'm playing and what I'm trying to do with the side.

'It's run by a clique of public schoolboys'

It is true that many of the leading administrators in English cricket were educated at public schools and Oxbridge but that does not seem so surprising to me. I would have thought that you need to be reasonably intelligent and have a good education to be a top-class administrator. And since many of these people got into first-class cricket through Oxford and Cambridge it seems sensible that they should have stayed in the game.

Oxbridge cricket is perhaps becoming something of an anachronism as the universities struggle to put out sides which are up to first-class standard but I benefited enormously from going to Cambridge. I enjoyed my time there immensely and I would love to see them continue in first-class cricket – but only if they have enough decent players to provide the counties with reasonable opposition.

Times are changing and for proof of that you only have to look at the recent contest for the chairmanship of the England selection committee when an Oxford man in M. J. K. Smith was up against an archetypal northern professional in Raymond Illingworth. Illy won and M. J. K. may have been the victim of a backlash against what some saw as 'the Oxbridge mafia'.

I may be a Cambridge man but I also regard myself as a professional northern cricketer and while one does not necessarily mix too easily with the other I am quite happy to accept them both. It is too easy to compartmentalise people.

'Players don't seem to enjoy the game as much as they used to'

Maybe this is partly true. I remember reading about Denis Compton kicking a ball over the boundary to make sure an opposing batsman completed his second hundred of the day and I don't think that kind of thing would happen now. There is so much more at stake these days. Cricket is more cut-throat, there is more to play for financially and there is more criticism from the Press. To play cricket purely for pleasure is not as easy as it was. It is a shame but it does become more and more of a job as the years roll by.

To suggest that we don't enjoy it at all is absolute rubbish. We still have a lot of fun and plenty of laughs – like when David Gower went up in a Tiger Moth during a match in Queensland and came out to bat in the next game to the strains of 'Those Magnificent Men in their Flying Machines'.

For me, though, the greatest enjoyment of all comes from winning.

'They don't know how to tour any more'

This is connected with the previous question and, as I seem to keep saying, times have changed. England teams used to spend three or four weeks on a boat to get to Australia; for us, it's a twenty-four-hour flight. When they got there, they would travel around the country by train, giving them plenty of time to relax and unwind after a match and prepare for the next one; we can finish a floodlit match late at night and be up early the next morning to fly on to the next venue.

There is much more international cricket compressed into a shorter space of time because players do not want to be away from their wives and families for more than six months. There are also fewer days off. Most days are practice days, playing days or travelling days.

There are fewer opportunities to explore what a country has to offer – and when you are in a fascinating place like India that is a shame. And there is also the intrusive nature of the Press which prevents players enjoying touring as much as they did.

'Teams that are scruffy off the field are scruffy on it'

This probably goes back to the 1992–3 tour of India when the England team was criticised for being scruffy and I think that we were out of order on occasions. There was one presentation ceremony after we had lost the series in Bombay when we did look like a lot of ragamuffins but generally the criticism was unfair.

Once, we had been on a train for more than twelve hours travelling from Cuttack to Calcutta, arriving in the middle of the night and having to fight our way past the hundreds of people milling around Howra Station. To criticise us for not wearing jackets and ties was ridiculous.

Some people also made a lot of the stubble on our chins yet Mike Brearley, one of the best England captains of recent years, was not exactly a regular shaver and it is not something that I see as being particularly important either. I am from a different era, though, and it is something that Ray Illingworth and his fellow selectors do consider important, probably because they remember their National Service days. We therefore agree to differ, but naturally, since Illy is in charge and he wants us to shave every morning of a match, we comply with his wishes.

As for the way we dress, we do have regulations for every occasion and I do agree that players representing their country should look smart both on and off the field. I do not agree, however, that extra smartness makes for better cricket.

One of the most curious aspects of that Indian tour was that people were so busy complaining about our appearance that they did not seem to notice that we had been walloped 3–0 in the Test series. That is what we should have been criticised for.

'English players are all over-coached'

Our players are given no more coaching than players in other countries but I take the point that there are dangers in over-coaching – and particularly in poor coaching.

Coaching is important because it is vital for players to know the basics of technique but I would guard against too much of it at an early stage in their careers. What coaches have to do is teach the fundamental principles, without which a player will not succeed, but at the same time encourage natural flair and talent and, above all, promote enjoyment of the game.

Gordon Barker, the former Essex batsman, produced a stream of good cricketers from Felsted School and they say that what he had above all else was a natural enthusiasm for the game which he was able to convey to the players he was coaching. Lancashire's David Lloyd has that, too.

I am all in favour of coaching as long as it is of the required quality. Unfortunately I think the general standard of coaching in England is poor. It is very much a 'jobs for the boys' syndrome with players finishing moderate county careers immediately becoming Second XI coaches. Some of them may be very good at the job but others are not so impressive, particularly those who do not recognise what is inherently good in a player's game and encourage that.

The really top players often listen to no more than one person who they trust and believe in. Years after he became a Test player, Geoff Boycott would keep going back to Johnny Lawrence, the former Somerset leg-spinner, who had a coaching clinic near his home and had coached him since he was a schoolboy. The advantage of that was that Johnny knew Geoff's game inside out and would immediately spot any little errors that might have crept in.

There is a great danger in listening to people who do not know your game at all. When young Mark Lathwell got into the England team he suddenly found that his technique was being dissected in the media by people who had never seen him play. That is a dangerous scenario.

But there is no doubt that when you do get a top-class coach like Geoff Boycott working with a good player the results can be astounding.

OUT OF THE ORDINARY

33 UNORTHODOXY

Two masters of the unorthodox – (BELOW LEFT) *Viv Richards and* (RIGHT) *Ian Botham.*

Cricket would be a very dull and stereotyped game if everybody followed the coaching book to the letter and we all finished up with the same technique. The great players, the match-winners who tilt the balance in the big games and the entertainers who pull in the crowds, are those who defy the conventional wisdom and make their own rules.

It is fair to say that almost all the great players have two things in common – their orthodoxy and their unorthodoxy. By that I mean

that they all have a sound basic technique and it is their unwavering belief in that foundation which gives them the confidence to do the most extraordinary things.

Take Ian Botham who broke all the records as a match-winning all-rounder. He knocked the first ball he received from Australian fast bowler Craig McDermott in a Test match straight back over his head for six. Yet in reality it was a completely orthodox shot – straight backlift, straight bat, straight follow-through. It was only unorthodox in its boldness and daring.

Botham will be remembered for strokes like that, yet, when he chose to, he could play the most solid and watchful innings. He once blocked every ball of the last over of an important one-day game with the scores level because he knew that if his side did not lose another wicket they would win anyway. And he once helped to save a Test against Pakistan by playing for hours on end without a single false stroke.

Viv Richards, the greatest batsman of his generation, was much the same. He was totally unorthodox in his ability to destroy an attack by whacking perfectly respectable good-length balls through midwicket yet he could play supremely orthodox and responsible innings when the situation demanded it.

And look at Brian Lara, the greatest batsman in the game today. The basics of his technique are very sound. He keeps his head still, he picks his bat up straight and high, he moves his feet either right forward or right back. Yet he can be very unorthodox and many of we lesser mortals were amused when he began a coaching column for the *Daily Mail* and one of his first lessons was the whip through midwicket from on or outside the off stump. Now this *is* an unorthodox shot and very difficult to execute and it is only because he is such a gifted batsman with so much confidence in his technique that he can play it almost at will.

West Indians seem to be particularly inventive when it comes to unorthodox shots, none more so than Rohan Kanhai, another batting genius, who perfected the fall-over sweep in which he would literally swing himself off his feet as he deposited the ball over the boundary rope. It was not an easy stroke to copy but John Emburey, a born improviser himself, did it to some effect against Shane Warne and Tim May the last time the Australians were in England.

Other batsmen with fewer natural gifts, perhaps, than the Laras and the Kanhais have been unorthodox in other ways. Peter Willey, one of the bravest of England batsmen, developed such a two-eyed stance that he seemed to be taking guard from the square leg umpire while Middlesex's John Carr went even further, not only facing somewhere between square leg and midwicket but cocking his bat up around his ear. They looked strange but their methods worked for them, Willey earning the respect of the West Indian fast bowlers, no less, and Carr topping the first-class averages in 1994 with more than 1,500 runs at an average of over 90.

There have been other strange sights, like the exaggerated backlift introduced by Tony Greig and Mike Brearley and still employed by Graham Gooch. There have also been some unusual grips. Nottinghamshire's Basharat Hassan used to have one hand right at the top of the handle and the other right down at the bottom while Alan Knott promoted 'the Kent grip' with the back of his hand round the top of the handle facing towards himself.

Some of the greatest bowlers have been very unorthodox, too. Malcolm Marshall was chest-on when the coaching book says you should be sideways-on yet he finished up as the West Indies' leading wicket-taker. Lance Gibbs bowled his off breaks from wide of the crease instead of getting close to the stumps yet he was their most successful spinner.

John Gleeson, the Australian 'mystery' spinner, held the ball between his first two fingers and spun it by rolling them down one side or the other depending on which way he wanted it to go. Fast bowler Jeff Thomson had an extraordinary slinging action with which he seemed to catapult the ball from almost down by his feet. And now we have Paul Adams, South Africa's new left-arm wrist spinner, whose actions has been likened to 'a frog in a blender'.

They all defied the coaches – and why not? Cricket is an unnatural game. Batsman are told to stand sideways-on, keep the elbow high and play straight, but that is not natural. Ask a little boy to hit a cricket ball and his natural instinct is to swipe across the line.

It is only the great players who can be both orthodox and unorthodox and still make it look like the most natural game in the world. It is the rest of us who make it look rather forced at times.

34 CHANGING TECHNIQUE

Once they have developed their own way of playing, many batsmen are unwilling to change or modify their techniques. They prefer to stick with their faults and play within their limitation rather than risk losing everything.

Yet sometimes it is a good idea to have a rethink, as I discovered in the winter of 1989–90 when I made the only major change of my career – so far. These days we play and tour so much that you hardly have time to do much even if you want to, but that winter there was a three-month gap before we went away so it was an ideal opportunity. I had played in two Tests for England at the age of twenty-one and I realised that my game was some way short of the required standard so I turned to Geoff Boycott for a major overhaul of my technique.

The first thing he did was to tell me of my good points. There were not too many, he said, but at least he did tell me what they were. They included good rhythm and balance, nice foot movement, decent hands, solid basic technique, that kind of thing. The problem, he said, was that although I had good feet and good movement they were taking me into the wrong areas. What I had to work on was getting them to take me in the right direction.

Basically, that meant getting my right foot to move back and across rather than back towards leg stump so that I would play straight towards the bowler rather than towards extra cover and gully. Geoff had noticed that I had been getting out caught behind or caught in the slips and after working on it for three months I was a much better player the following summer.

That is an example of a major change as opposed to the tinkering that is always going on in a batsman's game. You find that if you are going through a period when you are out of form and not getting many runs you are always thinking about your backlift, your head, your hands or your feet. Usually there is nothing seriously wrong with your game – or at least no more than there was already – and it is all down to a lack of confidence. Now that I am more experienced, I try to get through these periods by just focusing on the ball and forgetting about all the other details. If you do that, you tend to find that your natural flow will return.

35 LEFT-HANDERS

The great thing about having left-handers in a cricket team is that they add variety. There are naturally not so many of them as there are right-handers and the very fact that they are different causes problems because they demand a change of tack by both the batsmen and the bowlers.

For that reason, it is always nice to have them although they have to be worth their places. You cannot pick them just for the sake of variety but the best ones are a definite boost to any side, as batsmen like David Gower, Allan Border and Brian Lara and bowlers such as John Lever, Bruce Reid and Wasim Akram have demonstrated.

Left-handed batsmen make bowlers change the angle of their attack, which is what Graham Thorpe did when he returned to the England side against South Africa in 1994. We had played them at Lord's with a batting line-up consisting entirely of right-handers and the South African bowlers were able to use the slope to their advantage by plugging away just outside the off stump with the result that we were given a real hammering.

We recalled Graham for the next Test at Headingley and although things were not exactly following the same pattern we were still bogged down when he arrived at the crease. Immediately the South African bowlers had to change their line and he carted them to all parts of the ground for a brilliant 72 and galvanised us into much stronger batting performances for the rest of the series.

Most of the bowlers I know do not like bowling to left-handers which, I would have thought, puts them at a disadvantage from the start. Just outside off stump to right-handers is obviously just outside leg stump to left-handers and that is meat and drink to them.

It is also an advantage to have a right-hander and a left-hander batting together because by taking plenty of singles and rotating the strike as much as possible they upset the bowlers' rhythm and composure.

There are one or two disadvantages for the left-handed batsman. With the natural angle of the right arm bowler taking the ball across them, they can be vulnerable in the slips and gully area – as my old Lancashire colleague Graeme Fowler will not need reminding. They also have to contend with a lot of rough outside their off stump

Graham Thorpe –
left-handers make
bowlers change their
line of attack.

created by the right arm bowlers' footsteps and it is the bane of their lives against the spinners.

Left arm bowlers add variety because they have a completely different angle of attack from the right armers bowling over the wicket. Whereas the right armer's angle is slightly in towards the right-handed batsman, the left armer will slant the ball across him towards the slips, inducing nicks towards the slips and gully. This can cause a lot of problems, particularly on bouncy pitches, and Australia's Bruce Reid and Chris Matthews have both done well against England in recent years.

To be consistently successful on all kinds of wickets, the left armer has to be able to swing the ball back in towards the right-hand batsman. It was his ability to do this that gave John Lever such a great record for Essex over the years and it is what his successor, Mark Ilott, is attempting to emulate

THE LOONY LEFT   No, I am not straying into the field of politics but referring to the unfortunate tendency of so many left arm spinners to lose temporarily – and, in one or two cases, permanently – just about everything that made them the bowlers they were, for reasons that can only be psychological.

It is like golfers or darts players getting the 'yips', that strange condition whereby they cannot make their putts or let their darts go. And it has happened to so many slow left armers that they must all be left wondering whether it is their turn next.

Why it should happen to one particular type of bowler is a mystery but few cricketers have lost their way quite as completely as Fred Swarbrook of Derbyshire, the late Ian Folley of Lancashire, Keith Medlycott of Surrey and, for a while, even Phil Edmonds of Middlesex and England.

The only explanation I can think of is that most of them had suspect actions – by which I do not mean actions that were suspect in the throwing sense but were susceptible to breaking down under pressure.

Keith Medlycott, who was seen as one of England's finest prospects when he went to the West Indies in 1990, had a peculiar action in which his arm seemed to come over the top of his head. Alex Barnett, of whom great things were expected when he moved from Middlesex to Lancashire because Phil Tufnell was standing in his way, had problems caused by the exaggerated leverage involved in his delivery.

It seems to me that it is a question of getting the basics right. If a bowler has a simple technique like Phil Tufnell, Richard Illingworth and Phil Carrick, there is very little that can go wrong. It is when you have a more complicated action with plenty of things that can go wrong that the pressure builds up and the co-ordination goes.

Yet that does not explain what happened to Phil Edmonds, a particularly strong-minded individual with an almost classical action, when he got the yips on a tour of India. He did not lose his action but his run-up went completely and he finished up just standing at the crease and propelling the ball from an almost stationary position.

BEHIND CLOSED DOORS

36 WHEN IT RAINS ...

When you play a lot of your cricket at Old Trafford, as I do, you get used to spending long hours *off* the field as the rain teems down outside. So how do we pass the time behind closed doors while the poor spectators huddle in the bars and stands?

It may surprise you to know that much of the activity is cricket-orientated and designed to improve our performances. Particularly in the early part of the season, when the weather tends to be at its worst, players will head for the gym to work on their fitness or the indoor nets to get in some practice.

There is all sorts of equipment in the gym at Old Trafford – weights, rowing machines, exercise bikes, that kind of stuff – and the players make full use of it. The fast bowlers might be in there doing a specialised weights programme to build up their strength and stamina. The batsmen will probably be concentrating on more arm and body work. And they will all take the opportunity to have their regular weight checks by the physiotherapist.

Some players might go for a run – at Old Trafford we have what we call 'the Chorlton Run' which is just over three miles – while others will do a few sprints out on the training field. I remember setting off for the indoor nets when rain stopped play in one of my early games for Lancashire against Notts and noticed that the great Sir Richard Hadlee was out there doing sprints even though it was absolutely throwing it down. It brought home to me that even a superstar like him was still totally dedicated to his profession and working as hard as he had ever done.

Quite a few players will go to the indoor school to use the bowling machine, to hone a particular shot or just to sharpen the reflexes. I will usually do that if I know that I am about to face an especially quick bowler and want to get my feet moving. Batsmen can also film themselves, either facing the bowling machine or playing against the net bowlers, and then go back to the dressing room to study the videos with the coach and talk about their techniques.

If all that sounds deadly serious, there are more leisurely pursuits. Some players, such as Phil Tufnell, just like to curl up in a corner and go to sleep. Most counties have a card school and I join in a fairly regular four with Neil Fairbrother, Graham Lloyd and Nick Speak – though not for big money.

There are also autographs to be signed and letters to be answered – especially since my appointment as England captain, which has brought a big increase in my mail. I am fortunate that the club has given me the use of the chief executive's secretary so I might pop over to the office to tackle some of my correspondence.

Some players are particularly methodical and well organised, with Graham Gooch an example to us all in this respect. And it does not have to be raining. As soon as he is dismissed, he will put all his cricket equipment away in a neat, orderly fashion and get down to signing his autographs and answering his mail.

I am definitely not like that. When I'm out, I tend to throw all my gear around so that mine is the untidiest corner of the dressing room. I will leave all my mail for three or four weeks and then try to do it all at once on a rainy day.

Finally, there are the crossword freaks like David Gower and M. J. K. Smith, manager of two recent England tours. He was so preoccupied at the precise moment of our famous victory over the West Indies in Barbados that he was heard to ask: 'Has anybody got 10 across?'

37 FRATERNISATION

(BELOW LEFT) *Ian Botham and Viv Richards remained great mates even when they were playing against each other but* (RIGHT) *Allan Border cooled his relationship with David Gower in 1989.*

For the vast majority of people who play cricket, it is a social game. They play for fun and part of the enjoyment is to have a few beers together afterwards. But first-class cricket – and especially Test cricket – is not quite like that any more.

I doubt if Douglas Jardine shared too many cans with Don Bradman during the 1932–3 Bodyline series and I know that Clive Lloyd did not swap too many rum punches with the Chappells during the 1974–5 Australia–West Indies showdown.

But probably the most dramatic development on the social side was illustrated by the way Allan Border changed his relationship with his English pals in the eighties.

When Australia came to England in 1985, Border and his rival captain, David Gower, were great mates. There were plenty of parties and barbecues and 'AB' enjoyed socialising with the Gowers, the Bothams and the Lambs. Australia lost the series 3–1.

When Australia came back to England in 1989, Border and Gower were still the two captains but AB had a much harder, tougher attitude. Socialising, fraternising with the enemy, if you like, was definitely out. And Australia won the series 4–0.

How much the changed relationship had to do with the difference in the results is hard to judge. What I would say, however, is that when a captain takes over a side he looks at areas which he thinks need improving. And when I took over as England captain I thought that we seemed to have become a soft touch over the years and needed hardening up.

I was thinking specifically in terms of cricket. We needed to be harder to beat in tight situations, such as when we had to buckle down and tough it out for a draw. And with that thinking came a feeling that we didn't want to be fraternising with the enemy and getting too matey with the opposition.

I don't mind players getting together off the field for a beer, a chat and a laugh but it can sometimes be awkward. Mike Gatting is very much in the old 'play the game – have a drink' school but when he came back into the England side in the 1993 Ashes series we were having such a bad time that none of us really felt like having a beer with the opposition. Even if we had a good day, we felt that we couldn't go and join them because it would have looked as if we were gloating.

I found it interesting that my thoughts about England needing to harden their attitude were in direct contrast to Mark Taylor's outlook when he took over the Australian captaincy from Allan Border. They had been heavily criticised for being *too* tough and he wanted a softer, more caring approach from his players. He didn't want them to play like pussycats, but he wanted to remove sledging from his side for a start.

My view is that it all depends on what you think your side needs at the time and certainly when we are facing countries like Australia and South Africa, who play it tough, I want to see hard-fought series with my English sides playing it tough as well.

In fact, I think Mark and I saw eye to eye on this at the start of the 1994–5 Ashes series. We wanted our teams to play hard but fair with the teams getting on well together but not going in for too much fraternising. During the series there was some fraternising. It was left very much on an individual basis. Players like David Boon, Ian

Australia's captain
Mark Taylor.

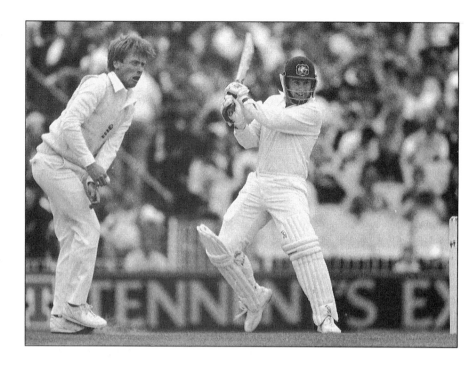

Healy and on our side Graham Gooch, Angus Fraser and Mike Gatting made regular trips to the opposition dressing room. As an individual thing I have no problem with that. Just as I have no problems with people like Steve Waugh and myself who don't make the journey 'next door'.

That may seem a shame but that's the way it has to be. The end of the series, when you've tried your best and you can't do any more, is the time for a beer or two. Then I will pick up a few cans, take them along to the opposition dressing room and have a chat about it.

❝ I wish to congratulate both Mark Taylor and Mike Atherton for the manner in which they have responded to the umpires' infrequent requests for them to control players on the field. I have had to act on several occasions for mainly minor breaches but seeing both teams applauding one another's good performances and witnessing the Australian's farewell gesture to Graham Gooch and Mike Gatting has impressed on me that the game is in good hands. ❞

New Zealand's JOHN REID, the match referee, after the 1994–5 Ashes series

THE GREAT DEBATES

38 THE GOLDEN AGE

There is no shortage of people who will tell you that cricket and cricketers are not as good as they used to be. Yet how can this be true when in every sport where performances can be measured, standards have improved beyond all recognition?

Runners run faster, jumpers jump higher, throwers throw further, swimmers swim quicker ... I could go on. Only in team games like cricket are we asked to believe that sportsmen have not even stood still but actually gone backwards.

People talk nostalgically of the Golden Age – which was, in fact, before the First World War so few of them will be able to remember it – and go misty-eyed over the sublime summer of 1947 when both Denis Compton and Bill Edrich scored more than 3,000 runs in the season.

I have no way of knowing whether the game was better then but some aspects of it *must* have improved.

Look at the equipment for a start. All the developments in bats, pads, gloves and footwear must have benefited the batsmen to some extent. Then look at the levels of fitness. All the improvements in training facilities and techniques must have given the bowlers more stamina and the fielders more athleticism.

Where the game has probably suffered is in its appeal to the present generation. There are so many distractions these days with the result that fewer people are interested in either playing or watching cricket. In the thirties, Roses matches between Lancashire and Yorkshire would attract crowds of between 25,000 and 30,000 to Old Trafford, Headingley and Bramall Lane. Today, we are lucky if 2,000 turn up.

Youngsters have more demands on their time from television, computers, and a whole new range of sports, mostly imported from America. Even in the West Indies, they are feeling the pinch. The popular image is of hordes of loose-limbed youngsters playing cricket on golden beaches and dreaming of emulating Brian Lara and Curtly Ambrose; the reality is that baseball, basketball, even football are rapidly taking over cricket's domain.

On top of that, cricket itself has changed, making comparisons highly dangerous and figures absolutely useless. A batsman's record is partly governed by the bowlers and fielders of his day, a bowler's average greatly influenced by the quality of the batsmen he bowled against.

Playing conditions vary enormously, too, so that statistics mean different things at different times. A batsman who averaged 40 at Old Trafford in the early nineties was considered to have had no more than a moderate season because the pitches were so good; a batsman who averaged 40 there in the mid-seventies would have been thought to have had an excellent season because the pitches were so green and uneven.

Just compare the career averages of current Lancashire players like Fairbrother, Crawley and myself with those of such fine players as David Lloyd and Barry Wood and you will see that ours are well over 40 while theirs are in the low 30s. We may be better players than they were but I have my doubts. And I am certain we are not 10 runs an innings better.

Factors like that are changing all the time. Fast bowlers used to be able to deliver the ball from much closer to the batsmen because of the old no-ball law which allowed them to drag their back foot. One notorious Australian dragger would finish up so far down the pitch that when Colin Cowdrey was advised to play forward to him, he said that he was afraid of treading on his toes!

The lbw law has changed as well. Once upon a time a batsman could not be out if he padded up and played no stroke to a ball pitching outside his off stump but now he *can* be dismissed that way.

Then there is the unarguable fact that the standard of fielding has improved beyond belief, particularly since the introduction of one-day cricket. The catching, chasing, diving and throwing are infinitely better than they were even when I started And that obviously makes it more difficult for batsmen to score runs.

All these things make some parts of the game easier and other parts harder and so distort the records that it is impossible to be sure about anything.

Other people's opinions are not a lot of help, either. I go into England selection meetings and hear Messrs Illingworth and Titmus complaining about the poor standard of county cricket – yet Keith Fletcher used to tell me that in the sixties and seventies there were only two or three counties who ever thought they could win anything. The rest were there just to make up the numbers.

Nor is video evidence that reliable. Fred Trueman always says that the black and white pictures make him look slower than he actually was! And though Harold Larwood on film looks sharp enough to me, the other members of the supposed four-man pace attack do not look so quick.

All we can be sure about, I think, is that the records and the reputations of the truly great players will stand the test of time.

Sir Donald Bradman, for instance, averaged 99.94 in Tests and 95.14 in all first-class matches and that is so far ahead of anybody else that he had to be the greatest batsman of them all.

Interestingly, I was talking in 1990–1 to Barry Richards, one of the greatest of the more modern players, and he said he thought that Bradman's average of 56.57 in the Bodyline series was about what it would have been if he had had to play against the fearsome West Indian attack of recent years. That may well be right but most batsmen would settle for that!

Apart from Bradman, who stands on a pedestal, I believe that all the other 'great' players of yesterday would have been great in any era. Equally, I believe that the great players of today like Lara, Ambrose and Warne would have been just as great twenty, fifty or a hundred years ago.

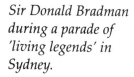

Sir Donald Bradman during a parade of 'living legends' in Sydney.

39 OVERSEAS PLAYERS

If anyone doubts the value of overseas players in English cricket, they have only got to look at the impact Brian Lara made in his first season with Warwickshire in 1994. Apart from scoring more than 2,000 runs, including a world record 501 not out, he inspired them to win three of the four domestic competitions, attracted almost 2,000 new members and doubled their attendances in both the County Championship and the Sunday League.

Not every county has been so lucky – and Warwickshire *were* lucky in that they only signed the world's best batsman after their original choice, the Indian all-rounder Manoj Prabhakar, had failed a fitness check – and the Test and County Cricket Board is currently locked in debate over its future imports policy.

There was some talk of doing without them altogether because with the addition of South Africa, Sri Lanka and Zimbabwe to Test cricket extending the international programme many stars were having to go and play for their countries before the end of the English season and many counties were worried that they were not getting value for money.

There is no doubt, however, that the overseas players gave the county game a great boost when English cricket first opened its doors to them in 1968 and I think that they still do more good than harm.

There used to be no limit to how many a county could sign and clubs like Gloucestershire (with Mike Procter, Zaheer Abbas and Sadiq Mohammad) and Warwickshire (with Rohan Kanhai, Lance Gibbs and Khalid Ibadulla) would regularly field three in one side , which must have affected the development of young English players.

Now counties are limited to one each and I think that is perfectly reasonable although the arguments over the pros and cons of having them in English cricket at all continue. They go something like this ...

FOR ...

Increased revenue

By signing a world-class player, a county is likely to attract more members, more spectators paying at the gate and more sponsors. Just look at the Lara effect.

Entertainment Value

Many of the overseas players have been truly great players, from Sir Gary Sobers and Barry Richards, who were among the first intake, to

Brian Lara. Look at the impact he made as an overseas player.

Clive Lloyd and Viv Richards to Curtly Ambrose and Brian Lara. They have brought tremendous flair and rich entertainment value to the county game.

The challenge

The overseas players provide a stiff challenge for any home-grown cricketer who wants to know how good he is. Without the imports, our players would not be tested to the highest standards. When a batsman has to face a bowler of Ambrose's calibre he gets some idea of what Test cricket is all about.

Raising standards

Overseas players do a good job in raising the general standard of county cricket. There are so many counties that English talent is thinly spread and the stars go some way to maintaining the overall quality.

Worldwide improvement

English cricket has the only professional structure in the world and this has played an important part in the general improvement in standards throughout the world. Players come from Australia, New

Zealand, South Africa, the West Indies and the Sub-Continent to play in league and county cricket and they go home as better cricketers.

Showing the way

It is every county's fervent hope that their overseas star will help their younger players along and there is plenty of evidence to suggest that they do. Micky Roseberry, who left Middlesex to become captain of Durham, learned an enormous amount from batting with Desmond Haynes, and Brian Lara's influence on Warwickshire's Roger Twose was quite staggering. In 1993, his batting average was 12.44; in 1994, it was 55.80.

AGAINST ...
Counter-productive

One of the biggest arguments against overseas players is that they use our game to improve their cricket and then come back here with their own Test sides and help them to beat us. Fast bowlers like Anderson Cummins and Cameron Cuffy have gained valuable experience in county cricket with Durham and Surrey respectively and will no doubt use it against us when they play for the West Indies. It is also slightly irritating that Australia will send up-and-coming players like Michael Kasprowicz and Michael Bevan to Essex and Yorkshire respectively to further their cricket educations but will not let their established stars come for fear of burn-out.

They're lazy

Some overseas players have turned out to be lazy cricketers and have not put as much effort into their cricket or as many hours into coaching the youngsters as their counties would have hoped. But they pay their money and they take their choice – so it's up to them what they get.

Pay demands

Since agents have come into the game, the money the overseas players are demanding is far in excess of what the best English players are getting – and sometimes double the amount. Counties are beginning to wonder whether they are worth it.

Over-dependence

There is a feeling that English cricket is becoming too dependent on the overseas players. In the leagues, any club wanting to win a championship or chase promotion will immediately look to recruit an overseas player to help them do it instead of looking at their own talent and using the money to improve the club's structure. In county cricket, Lancashire were without Wasim Akram for much of the 1994 season and their younger bowlers, Peter Martin and Glen Chapple, took on extra responsibility to finish with 50 wickets apiece for the first time.

This suggests that with fewer overseas stars, young English players would get more opportunity although this is a somewhat bland argument because there are so many openings in county cricket that the young players will come through anyway.

❝ Without overseas players, the English county game would be dead. ❞

SIR RICHARD HADLEE

---

40 BALL-TAMPERING

Ball-tampering – or 'Changing the Condition of the Ball', as the Laws of Cricket have it – has become one of the most controversial issues in the game in recent times.

This is mainly because of the relatively new phenomenon of 'reverse-swing', which first came to prominence on the Sub-Continent. There, on hard, dry pitches and rough, sun-baked outfields the ball soon loses its seam and shine and will not swing in the conventional manner. The bowlers discovered that by keeping the ball rough and scuffed on one side and smooth and shiny on the other they could get it to swing in the direction of the shiny side (the reverse of the normal swing pattern).

The first exponent of this was supposed to be Sarfraz Nawaz, the former Pakistan and Northamptonshire bowler, who passed on his discovery to the next generation of Pakistan – and, presumably, Northants – bowlers and now the technique is being copied all round the world.

What makes it so controversial is that some people have admitted that balls have been tampered with to assist in the process. Imran Khan, the former Pakistan captain, who also played for Worcestershire and Sussex, has confessed that he used a bottle top at some stage of his career and the New Zealand cricket team admitted that they did something similar in a Test match in Pakistan when their fast medium bowler, Chris Pringle, took eleven wickets.

Imran Khan discusses the condition of the ball with umpire Barrie Meyer during a Test match at Headingley.

There is nothing new in players trying to alter the condition of the ball. They have been 'picking the seam' – in other words lifting it with a thumb nail so that it protrudes above the surface and helps the ball to deviate one way or the other – since the game began. And they have used all kinds of agents like hair oil, sun cream and lip salve to improve the shine and make it swing.

But the fact of the matter is that such practices are against the Laws. They are covered by Law 42 which relates to Unfair Play.

Lifting the seam

Law 42 (4) states:

A player shall not lift the seam of the ball for any reason. Should this be done, the umpires shall change the ball for one of similar condition to that in use prior to the contravention.

Changing the condition of the ball

Law 42 (5) goes on:

Any member of the fielding side may polish the ball provided that such polishing wastes no time and that no artificial substance is used. No one shall rub the ball on the ground or use any artificial substance or take any other action to alter the condition of the ball.

In the event of a contravention of the Law, the umpires, after consultation, shall change the ball for one of similar condition to that in use prior to the contravention.

This Law does not prevent a member of the fielding side from drying a wet ball, or removing mud from the ball.

Further to these Laws, the TCCB has introduced a condition whereby the umpire at the striker's end must inspect the ball at the end of each over. The umpires are also required to make 'further frequent and irregular inspections'.

So what, may you ask, is the problem? I am not alone in thinking that the Laws should be changed to allow certain actions which the players tacitly accept as part and parcel of the game.

What, as Imran Khan asked recently, is wrong with lifting a seam which was prominent when the ball was new but has become flattened after 40 overs? Why should players not rub the ball in the bowler's footholds, which used to be allowed, or use their fingers to keep one side of the ball dry, as I was seen to do at Lord's in 1994?

I think that Sir Richard Hadlee spoke a lot of sense when he said in his column in a New Zealand newspaper that the time has come to 'legalise' ball-tampering.

'There have been subtle ways over the years of mucking about with the ball that allow it to do things like reverse swing after 40 or 50 overs and take the batsman by surprise,' he wrote. 'As long as the bowlers or fielders use whatever means they have on their persons, I don't see anything wrong with it. I'm talking about the use of a finger nail to scratch the ball, not bottle tops or those sorts of things.'

I am not suggesting that anyone should flout the Laws as they stand at the moment but I have to say that I agree with Sir Richard. I believe that if the Laws were changed it would help to provide a better balance between bat and ball.

❝ I always carried powdered resin in my pocket and when the umpire wasn't looking lifted the seam for Jack Gregory and Ted McDonald. ❞

ARTHUR MAILEY, Australian leg spinner in the 1920s

New Zealand's Chris Pringle – took eleven wickets against Pakistan.

41 THROWING

This is another emotive subject because if you accuse a bowler of throwing you are implying that he is a cheat – and sometimes that is far from the truth. Some bowlers have tried desperately to remodel their actions to make them legal but have been unable to do so for technical or even physical reasons.

At least the Laws are fairly specific on this issue. Law 24 (2) states:

Fair Delivery – The Arm

For a delivery to be fair, the ball must be bowled, not thrown. (A ball shall be deemed to have been thrown, if, in the opinion of either umpire, the process of straightening the bowling arm, whether it be partial or complete, takes place during that part of the delivery swing which directly precedes the ball leaving the hand. This definition shall not debar a bowler from the use of the wrist in the delivery swing.)

In other words, an illegal delivery is one in which the arm is *straightened*. The arm can be straight all the way through or it can be bent all the way through. But if it straightens, then it is a throw.

By throwing the ball rather than bowling it, a bowler can obviously increase the pace of the delivery and, not surprisingly, some of the fastest bowlers the game has known have been suspected of being 'chuckers' at some stage of their careers, especially those whose 'quicker' ball was distinctly swifter than all the rest.

The problem with throwing is that you have to prove it because it can have serious consequences and almost certainly finish a player's career. And proof is very hard to come by. One fast bowler, who had better remain nameless, was widely suspected of throwing and the authorities made several attempts to prove it on film. But he always knew when the cameras were there and was very careful to keep his bowling within the parameters of the Law.

There was a spate of alleged 'chuckers' in the fifties and sixties, including the Australians, Ian Meckiff and Gordon Rorke, the South Africans, Geoff Griffin and Cuan McCarthy, and the West Indian, Charlie Griffith – all of them fast bowlers. But spinners were not immune from the condition. Australia's Keith Slater and Jim Burke were both called and so was England's Tony Lock who suddenly developed a devastating 'quick' ball – apparently after spending one whole winter bowling in an indoor net with a low roof! Now we have the Sri Lankan off spinner, Muttiah Muralitharan, who was apparently born with a bent arm and underwent scientific tests to try to prove that he did not throw after being called by two Australian umpires.

Harold Rhodes, the former Derbyshire and England fast bowler, who was called for throwing six times in one match, went to great lengths to prove his innocence and finally convinced the MCC that the abnormality in his action was caused by a 'hyper-extended arm'. And Geoff Cope, the Yorkshire off-spinner whose action was twice declared illegal, remodelled it so successfully that he went on two England tours to the Sub-Continent before renewed suspicion persuaded him to call it a day.

That is the worst thing about throwing. It is very distressing to be accused of it if you are innocent – or, indeed, not doing it deliberately – and Phil Tufnell was justifiably upset when allegations of throwing were made against him in New Zealand. He does occasionally have a bent arm in his delivery but the critical point is that his arm stays bent throughout and does not straighten.

&& If they rewrite the Laws and say that double-jointed people must not be allowed to play the first-class game, well, fair enough. ""

Derbyshire fast bowler HAROLD RHODES after being accused of throwing

&& Put Burke on – he can throw straight! ""

Barracker on the Sydney Hill during England's 1958–9 tour of Australia

42 INTIMIDATION

Bowlers have been intimidating batsmen ever since the infamous Bodyline tour of 1932–3 when the England captain, Douglas Jardine, devised a plan to deal with the Australian batting phenomenon called Don Bradman.

It involved the use of four fast bowlers – Harold Larwood, Bill

Voce, Bill Bowes and Gubby Allen, although in the event the latter refused to have anything to do with it – bowling short-pitched deliveries to a ring of close fielders on the legside . 'Leg theory', as it was called in the best circles, worked to the extent that England won the series 4–1 but it damaged Anglo–Australian relations for years to come.

There was not quite the same kind of outcry but there were plenty of howls of indignation in the seventies when the West Indies launched a four-man fast bowling battery which put them on top of the cricket world and has kept them there to this day.

They had the fast bowlers to do it – a constant procession of them including Andy Roberts, Michael Holding, Colin Croft, Joel Garner, Patrick Patterson, Malcolm Marshall, Courtney Walsh, Curtly Ambrose and Ian Bishop – and this enabled them to maintain a constant bombardment which offers the batsmen no respite.

This was Clive Lloyd's answer to the pounding his team had taken from Dennis Lillee and Jeff Thomson, aided and abetted by Gary Gilmour and Max Walker, in Australia in 1975–6 when they were thrashed 5–1. Lloyd vowed that it would never happen to his team again and he kept his word – but while spectators thrilled to the spectacle of four fast bowlers going flat out all day, many of them were still appalled by the degree of intimidation involved.

There *is* a law which is supposed to deal with this kind of thing. It is Law 42 (8) and it says:

The Bowling of Fast Short-pitched Balls

The bowling of fast short-pitched balls is unfair if, in the opinion of the umpire at the bowler's end, it constitutes an attempt to intimidate the striker. (As a guide, a fast short-pitched ball is one which pitches short and passes, or would have passed, above the shoulder height of the striker standing in a normal batting stance at the crease.)

Umpires shall consider intimidation to be the deliberate bowling of fast short-pitched balls which by their length, height and direction are intended or likely to inflict physical injury on the striker. The relative skill of the striker shall be taken into consideration.

It goes on to say that if, after an initial caution and a final warning, a bowler continues to contravene the law, he will be taken off and not allowed to bowl for the rest of the innings.

Now I have seen countless instances of intimidatory bowling as defined by this Law but I know of only *one* instance in a match I have played in where a bowler has been warned and subsequently taken off. I remember it well because I was the batsman and Devon

Devon Malcolm – the only bowler I have seen taken off for intimidatory bowling.

Malcolm was the bowler in a match between Lancashire and Derbyshire at Old Trafford in 1988. The umpire, Alan Whitehead, stepped in and had Devon taken off because he was bowling four or five bouncers an over.

Most umpires just will not step in like that. I make no apologies for mentioning again what happened at Sabina Park in 1994 when Courtney Walsh tried to soften up Devon Malcolm. When Courtney pitched a couple of balls up, Devon whacked him for four. Courtney responded by bowling faster and shorter and then, when Devon started to back away, he followed him by deliberately firing the ball two or three yards wide of leg stump.

That was blatant intimidation of a batsman who was unable to defend himself yet the umpire did nothing about it. I don't blame the bowler, Courtney Walsh, who felt miffed that every time he pitched it up Devon whacked it, but I do feel the umpire ought to have stepped in.

Earlier in the same match, I had been on the receiving end of something similar from Courtney but I had no complaints because I am a frontline batsman and I am capable of defending myself.

Where the Law is inadequate in that situation, however, is that it defines a bouncer as a fast short-pitched ball which passes above *shoulder* height. Courtney is such a fine bowler that every ball was coming at me between the *ribs* and the *throat* and the law does not consider them to be bouncers at all.

The umpire could still consider them to be intimidatory but with the one bouncer per over rule, which was in existence then, and the two bouncers per over rule which applies now, he is not going to intervene over deliveries which do not meet the precise definition.

At least the new restrictions on bouncers prevent the kind of free-for-alls we have had in the past, such as when England's batsmen were being terrorised by Lillee and Thomson in 1974–5 and John Edrich and Brian Close were subjected to a quite brutal battering by the West Indies at Old Trafford in 1976.

But restricting the number of bouncers in an over is not the answer to intimidation. In fact I think that two per over is a better rule than one because it is less artificial – although there is a danger that it could lead to the kind of mayhem we have had in the past.

❝There are two teams out there; one is trying to play cricket and the other is not.❞

BILL WOODFULL, Australia's captain during the Bodyline series

❝There's no rule against bowling fast.❞

West Indies captain CLIVE LLOYD on his four-man pace attack

BEAMERS

For all the talk about fast SHORT deliveries, they are not as dangerous as fast HIGH deliveries or BEAMERS – defined in the Laws as 'fast high full pitches that pass or would have passed [if they haven't hit you between the eyes, presumably!] on the full above waist height of a batsman standing upright at the crease.' They are dealt with very severely – and rightly so.

It is often difficult to know whether the ball has slipped out of the bowler's hand or whether he has bowled a beamer deliberately – they usually apologise anyway! – but the law makes no allowances. Indeed, from 1995, English cricket has regarded *any* high full-pitched ball, regardless of its pace, as a beamer.

This is as it should be. Beamers are a nightmare to face because you are looking for the ball to leave the bowler's hand and hit the pitch and suddenly it is there right in front of your eyes, making it impossible to get out of the way.

43 THE PRESS

It is an ever-increasing part of the captain's job in international cricket to deal with the Press and what I try to do is talk to them both before and after a Test match when you can be facing around thirty or forty people.

What makes it that much harder for an England captain is that we have a tabloid element which is renowned for its fierce and at times fairly unpleasant criticism of the side.

Most players will accept criticism of their cricket when things go wrong. If we play badly and get beaten, that is fair. But there are times when our Press goes overboard. Take the 1994–5 tour of Australia when one tabloid newspaper printed the fax number of the team's hotel and invited its readers to tell our team manager, Keith Fletcher, what they thought of the side. I think that kind of thing is completely out of order.

The broadsheet Press offers the more acceptable face of the British media but a problem I have found with both sections is that you often find yourself talking to them at the end of a match when you are just coming off either a victory or a defeat; the adrenalin is still flowing and you are not quite as calm as you should be.

This is when I have made most of my mistakes with the Press, particularly when I had a go at them after we had beaten the West Indies in Barbados and when I referred to 'the gutter Press' after I had got out for 99 at Headingley in the aftermath of the 'ball tampering' incident at Lord's.

They were major blunders because it is impossible to take the Press on. Certainly with the tabloids you have to take the stick – and take it lying down.

My philosophy as England captain is to try to be as open, as honest and as helpful with the Press as possible and I thought we had a really good relationship in the West Indies in 1994. It was tested the following summer between the Lord's and Headingley Tests when some of the hounding reached a ridiculous level. I could not go home for a week after Lord's because there were fifteen Press men camped outside and I had to change hotels three times to try to escape from one of them who was following me around.

Apart from that brief period, I think my relationship with the Press has been a decent one. Players are becoming more and more aware of their responsibilities in this direction and I went on a media relations course prior to the West Indies tour.

Preserving the image of the game and promoting it in a positive way is essential at a time when cricket is facing challenges from so many other sports. We have to keep our share of the market and we all recognise that the way we present ourselves to the media is increasingly important.

It is one of the least enjoyable aspects of my job because I am a fairly private person. The part of the captaincy I enjoy is on the field, dealing with the players and getting the tactics right. The rest of it, the kind of heightened exposure that I have, I could sometimes do without.

(RIGHT) *Three Yorkshiremen who made a hundred hundreds – Geoff Boycott, Herbert Sutcliffe and Sir Len Hutton.*

(BELOW) *Brian Lara drives John Morris for the boundary which took him to his record 501 not out at Edgbaston.*

RECORD BREAKERS
(UP TO THE END OF 1994 SEASON)

TESTS

Batting

MOST RUNS

		Tests	Avge
11,174	Allan Border	156	50.56
10,122	Sunil Gavaskar	125	51.12
8,832	Javed Miandad	124	52.57
8,753	Graham Gooch	115	43.11
8,540	Viv Richards	121	50.23
8,231	David Gower	117	44.25
8,114	Geoff Boycott	108	47.72
8,032	Sir Garfield Sobers	93	57.78
7,624	Sir Colin Cowdrey	114	44.06
7,558	Gordon Greenidge	108	44.72

MOST HUNDREDS

34	Sunil Gavaskar
29	Sir Donald Bradman
27	Allan Border
26	Sir Garfield Sobers
24	Greg Chappell
24	Viv Richards
23	Javed Miandad
22	Geoff Boycott
22	Sir Colin Cowdrey
22	Wally Hammond

HIGHEST AVERAGES

		Tests	Runs
99.94	Sir Donald Bradman	52	6,996
60.97	Graeme Pollock	23	2,256
60.83	George Headley	22	2,190
60.73	Herbert Sutcliffe	54	4,555
59.23	Eddie Paynter	20	1,540
58.67	Ken Barrington	82	6,806
58.61	Everton Weekes	48	4,555
58.45	Wally Hammond	85	7,249
57.78	Sir Garfield Sobers	93	8,032
56.94	Sir Jack Hobbs	61	5,410

HIGHEST SCORES

375	Brian Lara	West Indies v. England	1993–4
365*	Sir Garfield Sobers	West Indies v. Pakistan	1957–8
364	Sir Len Hutton	England v. Australia	1938
337	Hanif Mohammad	Pakistan v. West Indies	1957–8
336*	Wally Hammond	England v. New Zealand	1932–3
334	Sir Don Bradman	Australia v. England	1930
333	Graham Gooch	England v. India	1990
325	Andy Sandham	England v. West Indies	1929–30
311	Bobby Simpson	Australia v. England	1964
310*	John Edrich	England v. New Zealand	1965

* not out

Bowling

MOST WICKETS

		Tests	Avge
434	Kapil Dev	131	29.62
431	Sir Richard Hadlee	86	22.29
383	Ian Botham	102	28.40
376	Malcolm Marshall	81	20.94
362	Imran Khan	88	22.81
355	Dennis Lillee	70	23.92
325	Bob Willis	90	25.20
309	Lance Gibbs	79	29.09
307	Fred Trueman	67	21.57
297	Derek Underwood	86	25.83

MOST IN AN INNINGS

10–53	Jim Laker	England v. Australia	1956
9–28	George Lohmann	England v. South Africa	1895–6
9–37	Jim Laker	England v. Australia	1956
9–52	Sir Richard Hadlee	New Zealand v. Australia	1985–6
9–56	Abdul Qadir	Pakistan v. England	1987–8
9–57	Devon Malcolm	England v. South Africa	1994
9–69	Jasubhai Patel	India v. Australia	1959–60
9–83	Kapil Dev	India v. West Indies	1983–4
9–86	Sarfraz Nawaz	Pakistan v. Australia	1978–9
9–95	Jack Noreiga	West Indies v. India	1970–1

MOST IN A MATCH

19–90	Jim Laker	England v. Australia	1956
17–159	Sydney Barnes	England v. South Africa	1913–14
16–136	Narendra Hirwani	India v. West Indies	1987–8
16–137	Bob Massie	Australia v. England	1972
15–28	Johnny Briggs	England v. South Africa	1888–9
15–45	George Lohmann	England v. South Africa	1895–6
15–99	Colin Blythe	England v. South Africa	1907
15–104	Hedley Verity	England v. Australia	1934
15–123	Sir Richard Hadlee	New Zealand v. Australia	1985–6
15–124	Wilfred Rhodes	England v. Australia	1903–4

Wicketkeeping

MOST DISMISSALS

	Tests	Ct	St.	Total
Rodney Marsh	96	343	12	355
Jeff Dujon	81	267	5	272
Alan Knott	95	250	19	269
Ian Healy	73	231	17	248
Wasim Bari	81	201	27	228
Godfrey Evans	91	173	46	219
Sayed Kirmani	88	160	38	198
Deryck Murray	62	181	8	189
Wally Grout	51	163	24	187
Ian Smith	63	168	8	176

Fielding

MOST CATCHES

Allan Border	156
Greg Chappell	122
Viv Richards	122
Ian Botham	120
Sir Colin Cowdrey	120
Bobby Simpson	110
Wally Hammond	110
Sir Garfield Sobers	109
Sunil Gavaskar	108
Ian Chappell	105

MOST CAPS

Allan Border	156
Kapil Dev	131
Sunil Gavaskar	125
Javed Miandad	124
Viv Richards	121
David Gower	117
Desmond Haynes	116
Dilip Vengsarkar	116
Graham Gooch	115
Sir Colin Cowdrey	114

FIRST CLASS

Batting

MOST RUNS

	Runs	Avge
Sir Jack Hobbs	61,237	50.65
Frank Woolley	58,969	40.75
Patsy Hendren	57,611	50.80
Philip Mead	55,061	47.67
W. G. Grace	54,896	39.55
Wally Hammond	50,551	56.10
Herbert Sutcliffe	50,138	51.95
Geoff Boycott	48,426	56.83
Tom Graveney	47,793	44.91
Tom Hayward	43,551	41.79

MOST HUNDREDS

Sir Jack Hobbs	197
Patsy Hendren	170
Wally Hammond	167
Philip Mead	153
Geoff Boycott	151
Herbert Sutcliffe	149
Frank Woolley	145
Sir Len Hutton	129
W. G. Grace	126
Denis Compton	123

HIGHEST SCORES

501*	Brian Lara (Warwickshire v. Durham)	1994
499	Hanif Mohammad (Karachi v. Bahawapal)	1958–9
452*	Sir Don Bradman (NSW v. Queensland)	1929–30
443*	B. B. Nimbalkar (Maharashtra v. Kathiawar)	1948–9
437	Bill Ponsford (Victoria v. Queensland)	1927–8
429	Bill Ponsford (Victoria v. Tasmania)	1922–3
428	Aftab Baloch (Sind v. Baluchistan)	1973–4
424	Archie MacLaren (Lancashire v. Somerset)	1895
405*	Graeme Hick (Worcestershire v. Somerset)	1988
385	Bert Sutcliffe (Otago v. Canterbury)	1952–3

Bowling

MOST WICKETS

	Wkts	Avge
Wilfred Rhodes	4,187	16.71
Tich Freeman	3,776	18.42
Charlie Parker	3,278	19.46
Jack Hearne	3,061	17.75
Tom Goddard	2,979	19.84
W. G. Grace	2,876	17.92
Alex Kennedy	2,874	21.23
Derek Shackleton	2,857	18.65
Tony Lock	2,844	19.23
Fred Titmus	2,830	22.37

MOST IN A SEASON

	Year	Wickets	Avge
Tich Freeman	1928	304	18.05
Tich Freeman	1933	298	15.26
Tom Richardson	1895	290	14.37
Charlie Turner	1898	283	11.68
Tich Freeman	1931	276	15.60
Tich Freeman	1930	275	16.84
Tom Richardson	1897	273	14.45
Tich Freeman	1929	267	18.27
Wilfred Rhodes	1900	261	13.81
Jack Hearne	1896	257	14.28

MOST IN A MATCH

19–90	Jim Laker (England v. Australia)	1956
17–48	Colin Blythe (Kent v. Northants)	1907
17–50	Charlie Turner (Australians v. England XI)	1888
17–54	Bill Howell (Australians v. W. Province)	1902–3
17–56	Charlie Parker (Gloucestershire v. Essex)	1925
17–67	Tich Freeman (Kent v. Sussex)	1922
17–89	W. G. Grace (Gloucestershire v. Notts)	1877
17–89	Frank Matthews (Notts v. Northants)	1923
17–91	Harry Dean (Lancashire v. Yorkshire)	1913
17–91	Hedley Verity (Yorkshire v. Essex)	1933

Wicketkeeping

MOST DISMISSALS

	Matches	Ct	St.	Total
Bob Taylor	639	1,473	176	1,649
John Murray	635	1,270	257	1,527
Herbert Strudwick	675	1,242	255	1,497
Alan Knott	511	1,211	133	1,344
Fred Huish	497	933	377	1,310
Brian Taylor	572	1,083	211	1,294
David Hunter	548	906	347	1,253
Henry Butt	550	953	275	1,228
John Board	525	852	355	1,207
Harry Elliott	532	904	302	1,206

Fielding

MOST CATCHES

1,018	Frank Woolley
887	W. G. Grace
830	Tony Lock
819	Wally Hammond
813	Brian Close
784	John Langridge
764	Wilfred Rhodes
758	Arthur Milton
754	Patsy Hendren
697	Peter Walker

GLOSSARY

Agricultural	Rustic, swashbucking style of batting.
Arm ball	Spinner's delivery which does not turn but follows the direction of the arm.
Bat–pad	Edged stroke which goes off the bat and pad – or vice versa.
Beamer	Dangerous high full pitch which passes above the batsman's chest height.
Bodyline	Name given to England's bowling tactics on 1932–3 Ashes tour of Australia (aka '**leg theory**').
Bosie	Australian name for googly (see below) after B. J. T. Bosanquet, its inventor.
Bouncer	Fast, short-pitched ball which passes above the batsman's shoulder height (aka **bumper**).
Carry one's bat	When an opening batsman is still not out after the rest of the side has been dismissed.
Chinaman	Left arm spinner's version of a leg break.
Chinese cut	When a batsman aims to play through the offside and gets an inside edge past leg stump (aka **Harrow drive**, **Surrey cut**).
Chucker	Bowler who throws (illegally) rather than bowls the ball.
Corridor of uncertainty	Bowler's line on or just outside off stump making the batsman uncertain whether to play the ball or leave it alone.
Cow shot	Swipe to leg, usually finishing at deep midwicket – or 'cow corner'.
Dolly	Simple catch (aka **sitter**).
Fishing	When a batsman dabbles outside the off stump at a ball he should leave alone.
Flipper	Leg-spinner's variation. The opposite to a top-spinner (see below), it is an 'under-spinner' or 'back-spinner' which is flat in trajectory and off fuller length than the batsman thinks.
Gardening	When a batsman prods the pitch to repair marks or remove debris (or waste time or calm the nerves!).
Getting to the pitch	Moving the front foot right to the pitch of the ball, i.e. where it bounces.
Googly	Leg-spinner's trick ball, basically an off break bowled with a leg break action (aka '**Bosie**' or '**Wrong 'un**').
Half cock	When a batsman is trapped – and often lbw – on the crease because he has played back to a ball of full length instead of getting his front foot to the pitch.
Half volley	Ball beyond good length which bounces just in front of the bat, making it easy to hit.
Hitting on the up	Driving without quite getting the front foot to the pitch of the ball.
Inside the line	When the batsman misses the ball by playing inside the line so that it passes the outside edge. 'Outside the line' is obviously the opposite of this.
Leading edge	When a batsman turns the bat to play to leg and the ball hits the edge facing the bowler and balloons into the offside.
Nelson	Score of 111, considered to be unlucky in England. Double Nelson is 222, etc.
Night watchman	Late-order batsman sent in towards close of play to save a more recognised batsman for the following day.
Occasional bowler	Non-specialist, usually brought on as a last resort (or to give away runs to hasten a declaration) (aka '**joke bowler**').
Pair	Two noughts or ducks in the same match. A 'king pair' is two first-ball ducks.
Pyjama cricket	Derogatory term for night cricket in coloured clothing.
Rabbit	Batsman of little or no ability.

Reverse-swing	Technique of keeping one side of the ball rough and the other shiny to make it swing in reverse to the conventional manner.
Reverse sweep	Turning the hands and bat to sweep the ball through the slips area.
Silly	Dangerously close fielding position – silly point, silly mid-on, etc.
Sticky wicket	Rain-affected pitch which is very difficult to play on as it dries (rare since introduction of covered pitches).
Strike bowler	Wicket-taking bowler with a good strike rate – usually fast though not in Shane Warne's case!
Stock bowler	Accurate, reliable bowler capable of bowling long spells and keeping the scoring rate down.
Sundries	Australian term for extras – byes, leg byes, no-balls, wides.
Swing	Making the ball swerve in the air.
Tail-ender	Batsman who goes in low down the order.
Throat ball	Bouncer which rears towards the batsman's throat (a West Indian speciality!).
Top-spinner	Leg-spinner's variation which goes straight on with extra pace and bounce.
Two legs	My guard of middle and leg.
Walk	When a batsman gives himself out without waiting for the umpire's decision (very rare these days).
Yorker	Ball which pitches in the batsman's block-hole, making it very difficult to defend.

WHERE AND WHEN –
MAJOR DATES IN CRICKET HISTORY

1300	First apparent reference to cricket in Edward I's 'wardrobe accounts'.
1719	First 'county match' – Kent v. London.
1787	Formation of MCC and first match at Thomas Lord's first ground in Dorset Square, London.
1806	First Gentlemen v. Players match at Lord's.
1809	Lord's second ground opened at North Bank.
1814	Lord's third ground opened on present site.
1820	First University match – Oxford drew with Cambridge.
1845	First match at the Oval.
1848	W. G. Grace born.
1849	First Roses match between Yorkshire and Lancashire.
1868	Australian Aborigines' team visits England.
1874	W. G. Grace first player to complete 'double' of 1,000 runs and 100 wickets.
1877	First Test match – Australia beat England by 45 runs at Melbourne.
1878	First full Australian team tours England.
1880	First Test in England – England beat Australia by five wickets at the Oval.
1882	First Australian victory in England – Ashes tradition established by 'obituary notice' to English cricket in the *Sporting Times*.
1884–5	First five-Test series in Australia – England win three of them.
1890	County Championship officially constituted – Surrey first champions.
1905	First MCC team to visit South Africa.
1909	Imperial Cricket Conference set up with MCC, Australia and South Africa the founder members.
1926	India, New Zealand and West Indies admitted to ICC.
1932–3	'Bodyline' tour of Australia.
1938	Lord's Test televised for first time.
	Len Hutton scores record 364 for England v. Australia.
1948	First five-day Tests in England.
1949	Donald Bradman knighted on retirement.
1950	West Indies win a Test in England for the first time and go on to take the series.
1952	Pakistan admitted to ICC.
1953	Jack Hobbs first professional to be knighted.
1956	Jim Laker takes 19 wickets against Australia at Old Trafford.
1957–8	Gary Sobers breaks Hutton's record with 365 not out for West Indies against Pakistan.
1961	South Africa leaves Commonwealth – no longer member of ICC.
1963	Distinction between amateurs and professionals abolished.
	First limited-overs competition – Gillette Cup, now NatWest Trophy – launched.
1965	ICC changes title to International Cricket Conference.
1968	Cricket Council, Test and County Cricket Board and National Cricket Association set up.
	England tour of South Africa cancelled because Prime Minister refuses to accept team including Basil d'Oliveira.
1969	Start of Sunday League.
1972	Benson and Hedges Cup introduced.

1975	First World Cup staged in England.
1977	Centenary Test at Melbourne – Australia beat England by 45 runs (same score as first Test).
1977–8	Kerry Packer sets up World Series Cricket.
1981	Sri Lanka admitted to ICC.
1982	Graham Gooch leads first 'rebel' tour of South Africa.
1984	England 'whitewashed' 5–0 by West Indies.
1985–6	England 'blackwashed' 5–0 in West Indies.
1988–9	England tour of India cancelled for political reasons.
1989	ICC renamed International Cricket Council.
1989–90	Mike Gatting leads last 'rebel' tour to South Africa.
1991	South Africa readmitted to ICC.
1992	Zimbabwe admitted to ICC.
1994	Brian Lara scores Test record 375 for West Indies v. England and highest first-class score of 501 not out for Warwickshire against Durham.
	Australian captain Allan Border retires after playing 156 Tests (93 as captain), 273 one-day internationals and scoring 11,174 Test runs – all records.
1995–6	England's first tour of South Africa for 31 years.

DIRECTORY

INTERNATIONAL CRICKET COUNCIL

The Clock Tower,
Lord's Ground,
London NW8 8QN

Full members

The Cricket Council (England)
Lord's Ground,
London NW8 8QZ

Australian Cricket Board
90 Jolimont Street,
Jolimont,
Melbourne,
Victoria 3002

The Board of Control for Cricket
in India
Dr B. C. Roy Club House,
Eden Gardens,
Calcutta 700021

New Zealand Cricket (Inc.)
PO Box 958,
109 Cambridge Terrace,
Christchurch

Board of Control for Cricket in
Pakistan
Gaddafi Stadium,
Lahore 54600

United Cricket Board of South
Africa
PO Box 55009,
Northlands 2116,
Johannesburg

Board of Control for Cricket in Sri
Lanka
35 Maitland Place,
Colombo 7

West Indies Cricket Board of
Control
Kensington Oval,
Fontabelle,
St Michael,
Barbados

Zimbabwe Cricket Union
PO Box 2739,
Harare

TEST AND COUNTY CRICKET BOARD

Lord's Ground,
London NW8 8QZ

First-class counties

DERBYSHIRE
County Cricket Ground,
Nottingham Road,
Derby DE21 6DA
Tel: 01332 383211

DURHAM
County Ground,
Riverside,
Chester-le-Street,
Co. Durham DH3 3QR
Tel: 0191 387 1415

ESSEX
County Cricket Ground,
New Writtle Street,
Chelmsford CM2 OPG
Tel: 01245 252420

GLAMORGAN
Sophia Gardens,
Cardiff CF1 9XR
Tel: 01222 343478

GLOUCESTERSHIRE
Phoenix County Ground,
Nevil Road,
Bristol BS7 9EJ
Tel: 01179 245216

HAMPSHIRE
County Cricket Ground,
Northlands Road,
Southampton SO15 2UE
Tel: 01703 333788

KENT
St Lawrence Ground,
Canterbury CT1 3NZ
Tel: 01227 456886

LANCASHIRE
Old Trafford,
Manchester M16 0PX
Tel: 0161 848-7021

LEICESTERSHIRE
County Ground,
Grace Road,
Leicester LE2 8AD
Tel: 01162 832128

MIDDLESEX
Lord's Ground,
London NW8 8QN
0171 289–1300

NORTHAMPTONSHIRE
County Cricket Ground,
Wantage Road,
Northampton NN1 4TJ
Tel: 01604 32917

NOTTINGHAMSHIRE
Trent Bridge,
Nottingham NG2 6AG
Tel: 01159 821525

SOMERSET
The County Ground,
Taunton TA1 1JT
Tel: 01823 272946

SURREY
The Foster's Oval,
Kennington,
London SE11 5SS
Tel: 0171 582–6660

SUSSEX
County Ground,
Eaton Road,
Hove,
East Sussex BN3 3AN
Tel: 01273 732161

WARWICKSHIRE
County Ground,
Edgbaston,
Birmingham B5 7QU
Tel: 0121 446–4422

WORCESTERSHIRE
County Ground,
New Road,
Worcester
Tel: 01905 748474

YORKSHIRE
Headingley Cricket Ground,
Leeds LS6 3BU
Tel: 01132 787394

OTHER ADDRESSES

MARYLEBONE CRICKET CLUB
Lord's Ground,
London NW8 8QN
Tel: 0171 289–1611

NATIONAL CRICKET ASSOCIATION
Lord's Ground,
London NW8 8QZ
Tel: 0171 289–6098

CAMBRIDGE UNIVERSITY
Fenner's,
Mortimer Road,
Cambridge
Tel: 01223 353552

OXFORD UNIVERSITY
The Parks,
Oxford
Tel: 01865 57106

WOMEN'S CRICKET ASSOCIATION
41 St Michael's Lane,
Leeds LS6 3BR
Tel: 01132 742398

BIBLIOGRAPHY

Barclays World of Cricket
    (Willow Books)
The Book of Cricket Quotations
    (Stanley Paul)

The Wisden Book of Cricket Quotations (Wisden Library)

Wisden Cricketers Almanack (various years)